Where will my journey end?

Based on a True Story

Sarah Louise Rosmond

BASED ON A TRUE STORY

INTRODUCTION...

This is part 3 of my story, and it explains some of the hardest parts of my life, how I have found a way to accept my past and finally found a way to move on, and how I finally found my happy ending.

At the age of thirty, I would go through the hardest time of my life when my husband Stuart suddenly passed away, again I was left in this world by myself, but this time I had children to think about too. I honestly believed my wedding day would be the start of my new improved life, the birth of our son Harry was a fresh start for all of us, until one day my whole life was ripped out from underneath me.

Follow me on my journey as a young widowed mother and visit all the twists and turns I encounter on the way. Nothing has ever been easy for me really, but I stick to my saying that, 'Everything happens for a reason.'

I may not be proud of every decision I have made in my life, but I am proud of what I have been through and at no point have I given up hope that life can get better, not only for me no but also my children and the other people I hold dear. Those who had entered my life and stuck by me when I needed them the most.

I have surprised both myself and my friends with the determination and strength I have shown up until now, and long may that continue.

Just because we have a bad start in life, doesn't mean that we can't break that cycle and create a life we truly want.

The biggest advice I can give anyone is live for yourself. Life can be cruel, it can be hard, but it can also be rewarding, and no matter what you do, always make sure that your life is in your own hands, for you are the only person who can truly make yourself happy.

– Sarah Rosmond xoxo

ACKNOWLEDGMENTS

The main person I would like to thank is my partner, who has stood by me in this over the years and helped support me in my writing career. He believed in me, even when I doubted myself. His love for me makes me stronger every day, and without his encouragement, I may have never published my first book.

A big thank you to my cousin Jody who you will meet again in this book, she is my best friend and has supported me through this full process and continues to help me to this day.

A thank you to my family member who can look past my story and help me edit my books and proof read them. I know at times it cannot have been easy mentally or emotionally. I cannot express how grateful I am to him for his continued support.

Lastly, I would like to thank you, my readers, because without every one of you, my story would never have been heard. Knowing that my books have helped others, is all I could have ever asked for.

Your support is what helps me carry on every day, and I cannot thank you all, enough. xoxo

Other titles now available:

Part 1 - The Sarah Rosmond Story – My Life in His Hands

Part 2 - The Sarah Rosmond Story – A Mile in my own Shoes

Contents

A LOVE LOST… 1

DAD'S HAT…..10

SHARON…...20

MEETING THE MOTHER IN LAW… 34

THE LONGEST GOODBYE…..39

STEPPING INTO HIS DAD'S SHOES… 44

CARL, HOW COULD YOU?!...55

I NEED TO MOVE ON…..73

FRESH STARTS AND FRIENDLY FACES….....................81

MISSED OPPORTUNITIES… 87

LET'S TRY AGAIN… 96

DRINKING BUDDIES…..104

WHAT SHOULD I SAY? 113

DREAMS CAN COME TRUE… 119

A PLACE TO CALL MY OWN….....................................121

FATHER'S DAY…...128

BETTER OFF BACK HOME….......................................134

DATING DISASTERS…..142

ANNIE'S TAVERN… 150

EMOTIONAL BLACKMAIL…...159

FEELING ALONE AGAIN…...163

BACK HOME FOR A WHILE….......................................169

OLD MEMORIES…..176

CONFUSED AND USED… 180

HALLOW'S EVE… 185

STUPID MISTAKES, LASTING EFFECT… 190

WHY CAN'T I JUST SAY NO… 197

CUTTING OUR LOSES… 205

WHEN WE JUST SETTLE… 209

REPLACEMENT BABY… 216

IT WASN'T MEANT TO BE… 222

RELEASING BAD ENERGIES… 236

BOOK BOTHER… 241

SOMETHING TO LOOK FORWARD TO… 245

A MESSAGE TO MY READERS… 253

A LOVE LOST…

I am thirty years old, and I had thought I'd finally found my happy ending when Stuart and I got married six years ago. I know he talked about death a lot, but I didn't think for one second that I would be a widowed parent at such an early age.

Stuart doesn't deserve to be dead, he was far from the easiest man to cope with at times, but he is the most loving father I have ever met. Harry is going to grow up wishing his Dad was still here, whereas I am just filled with even more hatred for my own Dad. Why did Stuart have to leave me? Why is he not here for us? Why is it that the men in my life who deserve to be dead are just happily getting on with their lives when my husband's lifeless body lays on my bathroom floor?

The paramedics finally leave, and the tall one tells the female police officer who was just interviewing me that the undertakers have been called and will be here as soon as they can. I look up at the clock and it is almost six in the morning already. I have been asked by the police officer if she wants me to ring anyone, but I tell her that I will do it myself when everyone is awake. My Mum rings my brother Daniel who is looking after my little sister to tell him what has happened. She is in floods of tears, and it hits me how close even she was to my husband.

Rachel returns to the house just before seven with her Mum. Debbie is a mess and can't even come into my house. I think knowing Stuart is still upstairs is just too much to handle. Seeing how cut up she is, makes me feel a little guilty. Debbie and Stuart were together for thirteen years and had three kids together. She had known him for most of her life, and there was me, who only shared seven years with him. Seeing how cut up her and Rachel are I think is what is upsetting me the most.

I am angrier than I have ever been in my life and hurting more than I thought was even possible, while my Father is enjoying his new life, God knows where. I might not have been able to tell my story before, but today has proved that you can lose everything in one single heartbeat. I could die any minute and I won't leave this earth regretting not saying anything. Stuart is no longer here to protect me which I know sounds childish and immature, but he was my hero, he saved me from Greg and I felt like my past couldn't touch me when I was with him, now that he is gone what am I meant to do.

The undertakers come through my back gate, and I am ushered into Rachel's bedroom while the police escort the undertaker upstairs. Rachel is in floods of tears but the anger I think has stopped me crying. That makes me even more annoyed that I cannot cry. I am fucked up or what? I know it is all going to hit me soon, but I am grateful that for now, I can hold myself together for everyone else. I know I said I am a widow at the age of thirty but those poor kids have just lost their father. Rachel is almost eighteen and I hear every young woman needs her Daddy. I wouldn't know of course. Carl is only just turned seventeen and Elise is about to turn sixteen in a few months. These kids are far too young to lose their Dad. I start to cry again when I think of Harry growing up without his Dad. He turns six in two weeks, and I know Stuart had something planned, but he kept it from me as he said it was a surprise for me as well. Now we will never know what he was planning, but I must make sure my son doesn't suffer even though we know it is going to be hard. He is too young I think, to ultimately realize what is going on. Lucy, on the other hand, I am not looking forward to telling her that her daddy is gone. She had already lost one parent when Simon moved away and stopped bothering with her, now Stuart has gone as well, I am wondering how she will ever cope. How will any of us cope?

The police say their goodbyes once the undertakers have gone, and Mum has had to get back to my brother and sister, so Rachel and I are just sat in the living room in silence for ages. I then, make my way up to the bathroom, and I am left with the blanket they used to cover him, all I have left is blood stains on my towel. The paramedics said they put an incision into his throat to try and unblock his airway, so I am guessing that is where the blood has come from. I sit on the bathroom floor and cry silently for over half an hour. I then walk into the bedroom and see Stuart's wedding ring on the bedside cabinet. He would take it off every night because his fingers used to swell up in the evening, though I used to wind him up and say he took it off, so he could pretend he was single. He never liked me talking about him being unfaithful, even if it was all in a joking sense he would still take offense and go moody.

I break down again realizing that I will never see his sulky face again, or his big smile when I walk into a room, or even be cursing him for snoring all night long and keeping me awake. The realization that he isn't going to walk through that bedroom door again is too much for me to handle and I feel like my heart is going to explode as I try and hold the tears in.

I have no idea what I am meant to do next. I have never organized a bloody funeral before, and I don't know where to start.

First things first, I need to ring Stuart's Dad and tell him what has happened. I can't even see the screen as I try and find his Dads number, through the eruption of tears, that is suddenly escaping me.

It is surreal that just a few hours ago he made a joke about dying with a smile on his face. That was no smile, the fear in his eyes, and the panic on his face as if he knew it was the end. I am unsure if that image will ever leave my mind.

I am scared, how am I meant to tell a Father, that his son is dead? The phone starts to ring, and Malcolm answers almost straight away.

That must be the hardest phone call I have ever made but bless Malcolm; he was trying to hold it together for my sake. He did say that he would contact Wendy as he knows I haven't got my Mother in laws number. Malcolm knows that his son had issues with his Mother, and as much as Stuart told the kids and me that he never wanted his Mum at his funeral. He has no choice, and it is not as if he is going walk in and start a big argument with me.

Carl seems a little annoyed that Wendy has been called as he had been in the conversation with his Father and me whenever her name was mentioned. I hated the fact that Wendy had grandchildren who she never got to see and even more so since Harry was born. I have good reason not to talk to my Father, whereas Wendy and Stuart fell out over her not traveling to see Stuart on the day and time he had set for her. Stu was always very pedantic in that sense and gave his mother a deadline when she said she couldn't make it and could she come the following week, he had blown up at her and told her to never bother him again.

'The one thing Dad always said, was that she wasn't allowed to his funeral, so why you think it is okay to let Grandad invite her, is beyond me!' Carl snaps and walks back out of the room, storming up to his room.

'Ignore him Sarah, you know what is for the best,' Rachel adds.

I explain to her that I could never stop a Mother from seeing her own son, and that she gave birth to Stuart and deserved to be able to say a proper goodbye just as much as everyone else. Rachel agrees that I have done the right thing by my Husband as she knows herself, her Father had a habit of over exaggerating how bad things were between Mother and son.

Rachel heads up the stairs to talk to her brother and try and explain how inviting his Nan is the best thing that I can do, and it isn't even me, Malcolm is ringing his ex-wife to break the news to her. A few minutes later and Rachel is back down the stairs with me, and Carl has just stormed out of the door.

Great I think to myself, but I cannot blame him, I would be out of this door given half a chance.

It is an hour later when Malcolm rings me back to tell me that him and his wife Judy are on their way up to us, I know that it is a least a four-hour drive from Surrey to us. They should be here for about lunch time. I will need to get dressed and head to the shop because I have no food in, nothing to make lunch with anyway. We would typically do our big food shop on a Saturday but somehow, I cannot see me doing much tomorrow and the last thing I can think about right now, is food.

I decided to make myself a smoke and sit in the garden on my own for a bit. I am only alone for a few minutes when Rachel joins me and asks if I would like a coffee, I would love one, and thank her in advance. Rachel is so brave and apart from crying earlier when the undertaker had taken Stuart's body away, she seems to be coping better than the rest of us. She has always been very quiet at the best of times, but I need to keep an eye on her to make sure she is going to be okay, they say it is the quiet ones you need to worry about, and I am starting to worry already.

I feel the need to get out of the house for a while and ask Rachel if she minds watching the kids while I run to the shop and get bits in for lunch, she says she doesn't mind but I do feel bad for leaving her here on her own. Had Carl not have stormed out of the house earlier I wouldn't be feeling so on edge right now. I tell Rachel I will be no longer than ten minutes and head out of the door. It is mid-summer and very warm today, and this air seems really thick and muggy.

As soon as I see the shop, I am starting to wish I had walked in the other direction. We have this local store just up from Debbie's house, but we also have the local spar which hasn't long been built. The prices are higher in the spar but at least none of the staff know me, or my family. The shop I am walking towards is a local family run business and Raj and his family have known Stuart, most of his adult life. Raj forever wants to stop and chat with me and I am hoping he isn't in a chatty mood today. I haven't the energy to explain everything to him and would rather he hear the news from someone else. I am glad when I see his wife serving today. Tina is also Asian but was born in the United Kingdom, hence the very English name. Tina can be just as nosey at times, but it is normally my business that she shows interest in.

I have everything I need and make my way towards the till. I can see Victoria a few feet in front of me, she is one of Carl's many female friends and I am hoping she doesn't notice me. I really do not want to talk to anyone.

Tina is in a chatty mood today and starts asking how the shop is doing. I tell her it is going great and then she asks about the family. I am wondering if Debbie has already been in today to tell them but when I dismiss this morning's events and say that we are all good, Tina seems to believe me and doesn't push the matter. I know everyone has a right to know that my husband is dead, but I don't want to be the bearer of bad news. I have had enough of that today.

Malcolm and Judy get to us just before two and as soon as we have eaten, I am ushered into their car.

'Did my son have life insurance?' Malcolm asked.

It has just dawned on me that we have nothing, not a penny put to one side for emergencies or anything. Judy tells me not to worry and says that most places will accept payment plans anyway. My head has been so consumed with the look on my husband's face and those last few moments that I haven't even had the chance to think about this funeral.

'That is why we have driven up today, to help you sort all this,' Malcolm gives me a sympathetic smile and tells me that I am not in this on my own.

I am then asked what plans, if any did Stuart have in place and I go on to tell him all the silly rules he had. I explain that he wanted to be buried and even though he had been told that the chances were very slim, he had asked to be buried in the small church yard just up from the big kid's house. Malcolm asked how important this was to Stuart and I tell him that, even if that is the only thing on the list that we can sort out, that I know his son would be happy. Stuart didn't like big and fancy and that showed on our wedding day, as much as it was a good day we spent a whole four hundred pounds on the entire thing. A wedding on a budget, he would joke.

We head straight to the Registrar's Office to see what can be done and within an hour we have a humane service booked, as neither of us are religious really, and a plot paid for, in the cemetery where Stuart wanted to be buried. I am thankful that Malcolm has put his hand in his pocket and paid for both because from what he has said, it will be the chapel of rest that cost me the main bulk of this funeral. We haven't been able to set the date yet because we have no idea when they will release his body. I was told that, as this was such a sudden death, an autopsy would need to be performed to determine the cause of death. The paramedics had already told me they believe it was a heart attack but only by testing him, will they know for sure.

Malcolm and Judy head home just after five, they have told me to keep them informed and as soon as I have a release date, they will be back up to help me finalise the funeral.

DAD'S HAT...

After a long-winded conversation with Carl and Rachel, I am told that I am not to open the market stall for a few days. I have tried to explain that we need the income to live on, but I am told that between them all, they will get cover for us. I am a little worried that my business will be run by a bunch of kids and cannot chance the market management getting their backs up. I am meant to open the stall today, but Debbie had rung the market and explained what had happened. They agreed for me to take as long as I needed before returning to work.

Elise has just rung me to say that she is due home in an hour or so and has said she would be coming straight to our house with her boyfriend Will. They have been in a long-distance relationship for over two years now and this weekend was meant to be the time we all finally got to meet this boy.

Elise is smitten by him and had said in the past that she knew her Dad would love her boyfriend and that we would see why she fell for him, now

10

Stuart won't ever get the chance to meet his Daughter's first love, and William will never get to meet his girlfriend's Father. I am looking forward to meeting him finally, even if it is under the worse circumstances imaginable.

There is a loud knock on the door, and I am a little worried as I get up to answer it, whoever is on the other side of the door has covered the peephole with their finger, this is something I would do as well, so I can't be too frustrated.

When I open the door I can see Craig, he is my husband's best friend and it is clear that this man has been crying most of the day. I ask him to come in and offer him a coffee.

Craig said he needed to hear what had happened himself, as their other mate Frag had rung him with the news.

'I am sorry, I should have contacted you myself,' I say worried.

'Don't be silly Sarah, I just wanted to make sure you are all okay and hear from you what happened, that is if you are okay to tell me?' he looks like he is about to break down as I pass him his coffee cup. 'I am glad he had you, you know before all this.'

Craig has never told me that he was happy for Stuart and me, it is like he never really took too much notice, who Stuart was ever with, but I do know that Craig's wife Sharon, cannot stand the sight of me. She and Stuart had a falling out about three years ago now, and he had avoided her since, mainly because of the way she would talk to me, and about me to other people.

Stu had always maintained that Sharon was a jealous, overprotective friend and that the only reason she hated me, was because I was with him. I thought it was a little weird that she would act like that considering she and Craig had been together for over eighteen years. She was like this with any-one else in the past too, so it wasn't as if I was get-ting special treatment or anything. After years of this woman making her feelings known, my Hus-band had, had enough and argued with her. This meant that for the past few years Craig would have to lie to her and make up excuses just to visit his friend. I can almost guarantee that she has no idea Craig is here now. He breaks down as I try my best to explain yesterday's horrendous events, but I stay in Stuart's chair. I want to console him, but I don't, after all, he is a man and I am sure Sharon would have a field day if she knew I had my arms around her man.

As soon as Craig has gone, I head up the stairs to be on my own for a while. Harry is fast asleep on the sofa and Rachel has just taken Lucy to the park to give me a few minutes rest before the house gets crazy again later. My brother is due around tonight as well and I will be glad of his company. I have all the kids around me, but I feel so alone and empty. Daniel has a brilliant knack of cheering me up, though I know he is heartbroken as well. Stuart and Daniel had a fantastic bond, only really be-cause Stu loved his bad boy attitude, even though my brother would always say that he needed to grow up. I am sure he will one day but for now, I need my childish little brother to roll me a joint and make me smile.

I am asleep just over an hour when I can hear everyone down the stairs. It is Debbie's big bellow-ing laughter that I hear first, and it is so nice to walk up in a better mood. I still feel numb, but the anger is starting to subside now. When I walk into the living room, Carl gets up from his Dad's chair and tells me to sit down while he makes us all a coffee. Carl never offers to make me a coffee really, so I am grateful.

'I have kept your seat warm,' he said, 'I have told everyone that only you can sit in Dad's chair.'

I smile at my step son, just as I am about to sit down Debbie tells me that Elise will be back any minute as she has taken Harry and Lucy to the shop. I ask the stupid question that everyone asks in these situations; how is she? Debbie tells me that she is doing as well as can be expected but that she is beating herself up for being down in Gloucester with William.

'She wasn't to know this was going to happen, none of us saw this coming.'

'I agree a hundred percent and I have told her the same, but she won't listen. She will be okay though, you all just need time.'

It is Lucy I hear first running through the garden. Elise has got her a girl magazine which I know will keep my princess happy for a few hours at least and Harry runs up to me to show me his new car. It may only be a cheap one-pound car, but Harry started collecting cars last Christmas and must have over fifty of them by now. Each time he gets a new car, he is as excited as the last, and it is lovely to see both my children with big smiles on their faces. Harry has asked for his dad a few times today, and Elise tells me that he thought he was going to the shop to meet his Dad. I want to cry, but I keep the tears back for now. I stand up to give Elise a big hug and she tells me that she loves me. I am then introduced to Will. I have seen photos of him on Elise's Facebook, but it is nice to see him in person, I am surprised though as he is taller than I expected. I like him already and it is the way Stuart's youngest daughter looks at this boy that cements my decision. She looks on at him, in much the same way as her Dad used to look at me and it is beautiful to see.

Within minutes Daniel is here as well but he tries to tell me he will call back later when everyone has gone, Daniel hates crowds, but I manage to talk him into staying. He heads into the kitchen to make himself a drink and then rolls a smoke. I am relieved when he invites me into the garden to join him.

While I am outside it is agreed that Debbie and Elise will open the stall for me on Tuesday, I cannot complain as the market would only be closed for the one day and I am sure my customers' will all understand anyway. I Thank Debbie as she gets up to leave and she tells me that she has booked the next two weeks off work and that I am to lean on her for support.

To be honest, the next few days go by in a bit of a blur. I spend all evening watching TV until I finally fall asleep in the chair. My bedroom makes me feel sick each time I walk into it, but I cannot bring myself to tidy it up or change the covers, they still smell like his sweaty feet, but it seems to be the only thing that does still smell of my husband. Stuart wore lynx spray every day without fail but he had run out last week and I was meant to get him more when we were in Tesco's getting Rachel's bedding. Is it silly that now I wish I had bought it?

I told Daniel how I feel like I can't sleep until after two in the morning and he has agreed to come and stay for a few days and keep me company in the evenings. Carl is always out, and Rachel has been with her on-off boyfriend for most of the weekend, and not being used to having my own space to breath has me hating being on my own now. While Stu was alive, I had always hoped to just have an hour on my own, just some me time. He didn't like the thought of me sitting in bed and reading a book or watching my own TV show in the bedroom and would always go moody because he had seen it as a personal insult or something.

It is Tuesday and I have spoken to Elise a few times already this morning, I think in all honesty, Elise and her Mother are just ringing to check up on me. Debbie was asking how much certain items were, so she didn't over charge anyone, but I know one hundred percent, that every single item I sell, has a price tag and a label on them. Stuart was very particular about that one rule because he would panic a little if I ran to the newsagents or nipped to the toilet and really had a go at me for not having an angel figurine priced up. He was a dick and refused to sell the item to my customer, just to prove a point to me. So, I know for a fact, that every piece is always priced up. I have told Elise that I will be down the market for about two, I also need to pick up some paint while I am out. Daniel and Carl have said if I repaint the bathroom, it may make it easier for us all to use the bathroom again. Somehow, I don't see how changing colour will make much difference, but it is worth a try. I am up most of the evening anyway, so it will also give me something to do with my time.

The market usually is my own little escape from the real world, but as soon as I walk in through the big wooden doors, I am regretting coming here. The stall holders have been informed about my bereavement. The cake lady saw me first and was just laughing with one of her customers. Now she is whispering and looking very solemn. I would rather they act normal around me, and I make my way through the Market Hall with my head lowered. That is until George sees me, he is our local gay butcher who loved Stuart dearly, and they would joke every week about having a secret love affair. It used to make me giggle because my Husband was scared that George did bare some truth with his flirty banter. I would wind them both up, saying that I wished they would start an affair as it would make my life easier. Stuart, of course, hated me saying it and would give me a knowing look but I would take very little notice. Our local butcher has tears in his eyes as he tells me how much he will miss his friend and he offers to help me in any way possible, it is a nice gesture, but I cannot see me asking for help.

I am glad once I am outside the market, it is lovely and open, and even though it is busy every Tuesday, the fact that the sun is shining and the stalls outside are usually temporary market stall holders, I am being unnoticed, and I can blend into the crowd a little. I can see my market stall, but from where I am sitting, I know Elise and Debbie won't see me. I found this spot when I caught Stuart spying on me just because he had been told a good-looking young man had been at my stall twice in one day. The customer in question was getting a present for his wife who was eating at the café opposite my stall, he had paid for the item but agreed to collect it later that day, so he could keep it as a surprise. Stuart had a paranoid head at the best of times, but it did increase this past year, and in all honesty, it was starting to wear me down.

The Book man has just seen me and started walking over, I want to get up and walk away before he has a chance to say anything to me, but I can't be rude to him. Dave has been a good friend to the both of us since we first opened our stall, he is stuck in his ways a little, and it did take him a while to get used to my husband's sense of humour, but the past year or so, they had become very close. Stuart didn't have the same drive for the business as me, and I always said he only came to the market because he had made such good friends with the other stall holders. Dave's stall was next door to us, and it would be good being able to loan a book and return it when I had finished. Dave always refused to take money from me, so instead I would make him a cup of tea anytime I was making one for myself. The Blind man, called Simon had the other stall next door to us, he was a fascinating man who was a mountain rescuer when he wasn't selling curtains and blinds. Both men had been trading at the market for over thirty years, which seemed like a dream to me. I had always wanted my own gift shop, and Stuart helped me achieve my dream.

Dave has just given me a big hug. He then goes on to tell me that he has a new sign at the front of his stall and that he hoped I would come over and look at it. I already think I know what sign he means because of a few weeks ago, Stu was bored and decided to make some signs for our stall. He had made Dave a few as well but after seeing them, Dave had said that he couldn't put them up just in case any of his customers took offense. A few were a little offensive, but the one he has put up isn't all that bad. The sign shows a man sat in a chair, you can tell he is from the Victorian era by the clothes that he wears, and the large grand chair has you thinking the person in the picture is regal in some ways. The man resembles Dave down to a T, and even his hairstyle is the same. Underneath this photo, Stuart has added some text, saying that the book man has been at the market since they first opened the doors. That wouldn't have been possible as the market was first opened in 1244, and is one of the oldest running markets, in the whole of the UK. I love telling our customers the history of the Market Hall. I am right, it is the sign I thought it would be and I am grateful for the kind gesture, as I know how much he was against putting the sign up only last week.

Elise has seen me, so I head over to her. I scan my sales book and can see that it has been a quiet trading day, which is a bit of a surprise, as we normally do well on a Tuesday. I am guessing it was to be expected though. I tell Elise and Debbie that I had a phone call from the funeral directors telling me that Stuart's body is finally being released. Now we can sort this funeral out correctly. I need to see Stuart one last time, if only to say my goodbyes and try and remove this image from my mind. I hope in time I will forget the look on his face when he finally gave in to the grim reaper. It was clear that Stu was scared, but I have been assured that he wouldn't have been in much pain as he passed away and that he died before he had a heart attack. Stuart had a clogged artery that was stopping the blood flow to his heart. I have been told that even if he had got to the hospital that night, that there would have been a very high chance that he would still have died. Stuart would have had to change his lifestyle a long time ago if he wanted to live a long life. That has given me a little bit of comfort and stopped me blaming myself at least.

Elise is upset, the thought of seeing her father dead is too much for her to take in, so I try and avoid talking about him as such and start talking about how the kids need some clothes for the funeral.

'Can we take Dads hat with us tomorrow?' she asks pointing to Stuart's ridiculous Crocodile Dundee style hat.

We got the said item, while on holiday in Turkey. I told him at the time that he looked silly in it, so just to wind me up he had gone off and treated himself to it. I took the piss out of him for over an hour which just made him love the hat even more. Stuart would wear it around the house mainly, and you could always tell if he was going moody because he would bury his face in his t-shirt and put his hat on covering his eyes. One evening I had made a joke saying that I would burn the stupid thing and he acted like I had threatened to cut off his arm or something. Stuart told us that he wanted to be buried in his hat, but I didn't take much notice. Clearly, Elise had. I agreed that we could take it with us and asked Elise to bring it back with her later. We have planned to get the clothes shopping out of the way tonight because I have a feeling, we will have lots to do over the next few days.

SHARON...

It is midday when Craig and Sharon turn up at ours, Sharon had rung me up and asked if they could join us when we go to see Stuart at the chapel of rest, and I didn't feel like I could say no. Craig is my husbands longest friend. They have known each other for twenty-six years. That is not far off, the amount of time I have been on this earth. I envy those who have had long-term friendships. I moved about so much in my life that I was never in one place long enough to make proper friends. I have those who I was close to growing up, like Claire and Stacey but with no social media and no way to contact them over the past thirteen years, it was apparent that we would lose touch and never speak again. I have been thinking about my life a lot this morning. I realised that I don't have any friends and even Jody stopped talking to us after a fall out with Stuart, I would have loved to know why, but neither of them ever told me, and now Stuart isn't here, so I will never know. I had never realised until now, how alone I really am! Stuart didn't let me have friends because he worried I would be lead astray. That has me thinking about my dad, as he was the same. He hated me having friends but that was because he worried that I would tell everyone his dirty little secret. I am not sure why, because it isn't as if I would have told anyone, and there would be no point in ever mentioning it nowadays because even my husband doubted what I told him was the truth. He said he didn't want to believe me as it hurt him too much, but I think he just thought I was bullshitting like everyone in my past did.

Sharon was apparently abused by her Father too, or so she says anyway. When we first met, I was really annoyed when Stuart told me that he mentioned my past to Sharon, thinking it would help us form a bond. That wasn't going to happen though, as Sharon took an instant hatred towards me from day one. This week she is being overly fake, and it is starting to get on my nerves really. Craig is in the kitchen talking to Carl, while Sharon is hovering in the doorway, I offer her a seat, but she declines.

After a few seconds of awkwardness, I make an excuse and head to the downstairs toilet. I am only in there a few minutes when I give myself a little telling off. This must be hard for her as well, as she had known Stuart for just under eighteen years and met him when she and Craig first started dating. The woman is trying to make an effort with me, so I can least repay the favour.

My back is up, when I walk back into the living room and Sharon has sat in my seat, well I say my seat, it was always Stuart's and the kids had told me that I was the only other person allowed to sit on their Father's chair. I want to comment on her stealing my seat but instead I sit on the sofa and roll myself a smoke. Sharon reaches into her bag and passes me a tobacco tin.

'I wasn't sure if you still smoked it, but there is green in there for you,' she says placing the tin in my hands.

'Thanks, I do.'

'You can keep what is in there, I have loads at home,' she says.

I believe her too as Sharon smokes this weed all day every day. Stuart told me that the only reason she can afford to smoke so much is because she sells it to all the under aged kids who live near her. Again, that doesn't surprise me, I have been at her house when the dealers have turned up for their thousands of pounds at a time. Just knowing this has me happily accepting the contents of this tin. I am shocked though when I see that there must be at least fifty pounds worth of the stuff here.

'Sharon, are you sure?' I ask, but she just tells me to shut up and make one.

Carl walks into the living room and abruptly tells Sharon to shift her butt, he explains that it is his Dad's chair and only his Dad's wife could sit in it. I can see she is pissed off, but she hadn't dared say anything to Carl, not with the mood he has woken up in today. It is a gruelling day for us all, and I cannot wait to get to two o'clock. Stuart's body will be ready for us by then.

I have been to the shop and got a few bits that Stuart would have bought, two cans of lager and a packet of pork scratchings. Possibly the two main things that helped kill him off, but Carl asked me last night if we could put them in the coffin with his father and I didn't want to say no. I have a feeling that most will be a little surprised when they see that we are burying Stuart in his favourite ripped jeans and holey t-shirt, but that is what he had asked for, and I promised myself and the kids that we would honour their Father's last wishes, which includes how he asked for his funeral to be. Stuart even picked his own music, who he wanted to carry his coffin and who was or wasn't invited to the service. That reminds me I am meeting my Mother in law tomorrow.

We are waiting outside the chapel of rest for Sarah and Michael, they were leaving just after us, but Sarah needed to collect something first. Sharon is getting annoyed of waiting around, but in all honesty, I do not mind waiting. After all, this isn't going to be easy on any of us and I know it. Michael pulls up and it is clear that he has been crying, like Craig, Michael has known Stuart for most of his life, and they were close. I like Sarah because she was a life saver at mine and Stu's wedding and if it weren't for her rushing about the day before, getting my tiara, flowers, and cake, my wedding day would have seemed more like a funeral.

We are all ready and head towards the back of the building, I have already been into reception, so I know where we have to go. Debbie places her arm around my shoulder and gives me a talk about how strong I am. I can honestly say I am feeling anything but strength.

We all make our way into a big seating area, it looks like a private hospital with its large reception desk and potted plants, it smells funny in here too, almost clinical, but you can sense death is all around us. The hairs on my arms and the back of my neck stand on end as a woman walks over to me to tell me that they are ready for us to see Stuart. I don't want to go in the room, and I am so grateful that my Mum has Lucy and Harry because I need to cry, and I haven't been able to cry in front of them.

I take the lead, with Carl, Rachel, and Elise in tow. Elise wasn't with us the night he died, so hasn't seen her Dad yet. She needs to see him, so it all sinks in for her, and she had told me that a few days ago. I need this for closure so that I can get Friday nights' nightmare out of my head, and I need to see him finally at peace.

I have seen dead bodies before but seeing him lying in that coffin has my heart in my throat as I try my hardest to look at him. Carl put his arm around me as I hear everyone else enter the room behind us, I move to the corner of the room, allowing more space as the chapel of rest soon fills up. Everyone looks like they are about to break, apart from Sharon, she is just giving me the nastiest of looks. Rachel can see how I am being glared at and stands in front of her, to block her sight. I take a deep breath in before I walk over to the foot of the coffin. I reach into his old work bag and start to remove the contents to transfer them into the coffin with Stuart. First, I pass Carl the cans and snacks as he places them beside his Father, he says a few words and moves back away, tears are falling from his chin, but he still looks on at me with sympathy. Then I pass the bag to Rachel. She takes out a few photos of Stuart and the kids and places them at the bottom of the coffin by her Dad's feet. She manages to say, 'I love you Dad,' before walking out of the room, pushing past anyone stood near the doorway, Carl follows her. Elise hugs me before taking out her Father's hat, she kisses Stuart's forehead and then attempts to put on his hat. She struggles, so Craig helps by lifting his head. Elise tells us that it isn't fair and then breaks down in her Mother's arms. With the bag now empty, it is my turn to place some sentimental stuff beside my Husband, and you cannot get any more sentimental that his wedding ring, which has been around my neck all week and my own silver heart necklace, that has been around my neck since I was sixteen. At least he has part of us all with him, I think to myself.

I leave the room and can hear a lot of talking happening, now that I am not in there, Carl and Rachel are outside having a smoke, and I head out to join them.

'He looks peaceful at least,' Carl says giving me a light of his cigarette.

'Almost asleep,' Rachel says.

'Yeah but without the dreaded snoring.' I try and lighten the mood, but it just causes Sharon to glare at me again.

The three of us have just had a small laugh to ourselves, it is the first time any of us has smiled since this happened, but it doesn't go unnoticed. We are being glared at again. Sharon has this resting bitch face down to a T.

'Ignore her,' Carl smiles at me and I smile back.

That was mentally hard work, and as soon as we get back home, I am grateful that most people have left us in peace. Seeing Stuart lay there this afternoon has really brought it all to the surface, and I cannot pretend he is going to just walk into the room again, because I have seen him, laying there and I know he is never coming back.

Craig rings me and has asked if I would go up and see Sharon this evening, he said she had taken today badly and she needs me to sit and have a smoke with her and just talk. I agree even though a small part of me fears that she just wants me up there, to kick my arse. We really do have no love lost between us, she blames me for Stuart being funny with her, but the truth is Sharon has always been very jealous of anyone who Stu had been with in the past. He hoped that she would be different with me and to start off with she was, while Sharon believed I was just a temporary girlfriend, she tried with me, until she found out Stuart and I were having a baby. The woman even kicked off on our wedding day because she wasn't one of our witnesses. Even though I know all this, I am still feeling bad for her.

Rachel and Elise decide to come with me to Craig and Sharon's, while Carl and Daniel stay at mine to watch the kids. Lucy has been a handful this afternoon, being nine years old, she can sense that things are not right. I heard Carl tell the kids that their Dad is in the hospital because he banged his head, and now Lucy keeps telling her baby brother that their Dad will be home when the doctors fix him. I cannot bare to tell her the truth, but I know I need to do it, sooner rather than later. Stuart's funeral is in two days, and I have decided that I want the kids to attend with us, they need to be able to say their goodbyes at least.

Sharon is in her bedroom when we get to hers, Craig passed us on the driveway and said he needed to pop out. I was kind of hoping he would be here, just in case anything kicks off, but Rachel assures me she won't let anything happen.

Sharon looks a mess, she has just been lying in bed all afternoon but sits up as soon as I walk into her room.

'Sit down please,' she says in a softer voice than usual.

Straight away I am passed everything I need to roll a joint. Sharon tells me that I upset her today, and when I ask what I said to cause her offense, she doesn't answer. Instead, I get told that if I don't remember then that says it all. Well actually love, it says nothing if I have no recollection of what I was meant to have said. I don't want to argue with this woman, so I just apologise to her.

'You don't even know why you are sorry,' she looks at me as if she is waiting for my response.

I can hear Elise and Rachel in the other room, and I am hoping they come and save me from this woman's riddles, so I call Rachel into the bedroom, to see if she can remember what I had said to upset Sharon.

'Sarah honestly, you didn't say or do anything wrong today,' Rachel sticks up for me, while giving Sharon a lovely dirty look.

'Thank you sweet, that was all I needed to know,' I thank Rachel before she heads back into the bedroom with Elise and Sharon's girls.

After the initial awkwardness is out of the way, Sharon and myself start to talk about Stuart, she has asked me to explain what happened, and how he passed away. I begin to describe the events from the day before, about how he had chest pains and wouldn't go to the doctors.

'If he were with me, I would have forced him!' she states.

'I tried, but he threatened to divorce me if I kept on at him.'

Sharon looks at me with horror, 'I would rather you both divorced than him being taken away from us like this.'

I don't think I deserved that comment, but I know tensions are high, so I try and ignore it. Then she goes on and asks what I did to try and save him. So, I explained how Carl and I attempted to do CPR on him, but it was too late.

The bitch then went on to tell me that I didn't try hard enough. Otherwise, he would still be here. She really has no idea.

Sharon starts to tell me stories about my husband, stories about him as a young man, well before I had ever met him, and it is nice to sit and listen to her. We start to chat about the little things we will miss about him the most and as the conversation flows I am mentally slapped in the face. Sharon asked me if I thought my husband and I would last, had he still been here today and of course my answer is yes.

'He was about to leave you,' she looks smug.

'I beg your pardon?'

'Stuart told me he didn't want to be with you anymore, he said he was going to leave you, but was waiting for the right time,' she is smiling.

'Sharon, I do not know where you heard that rubbish, but Stu and I were stronger than ever, there is no way on this earth that he was about to split up with me!' I am angry and trying my hardest not to raise my voice.

'He was, and he told me himself Sarah, he didn't love you.'

'Why are you so nasty, you can see how cut up we all are.'

'Because you have no right to feel like this, he didn't love you.'

I want to slap her in the face, why would she be saying such hurtful things, I haven't even buried my husband yet, and she is rubbishing his name.

'Why would you even tell me this? Even if it is true, what do you get out of it?' I ask.

'I didn't want to tell you, and I have stopped myself up till now, but the truth is Sarah he was only with you because he couldn't have me.'

Now I want to laugh so hard. Sharon is ten years older than me. She has had seven children and looks tired and haggard. I know looks are not everything, but she hasn't got a patch on me, I still look like I am in my early twenties, if that. My small build and tiny frame gives the impression that I am a lot younger than I am, hence why Stuart hated me ever wearing makeup or dressing up. To him, I looked like a teenager if I make too much effort. Sharon needs makeup to look even close to her age. I cannot be horrible back to her though, as that would make me as nasty as her, but she really does have a cheek.

'Sharon, Stuart got with me because he loves me, I do not remind him of you, in any way. If anything, he always said I look like his first love, Beth Ingram. I look nothing like you.'

That has to be the nicest way I can put that, without being too insulting.

'He asked me to marry him.'

Oh, now I am getting pissed off, the lies coming out of this woman's mouth makes me almost choke on the air.

'Hardly,' was all I managed to say.

I start to place my things back in my bag, and there is no way I am staying here to listen to this rubbish. I hate the fact that Craig isn't here, I would have loved to have seen her say all this in front of her partner. Craig would kill her for talking about his best mate in this way when he isn't here to defend himself.

'Sharon, you really are something else!' I get to my feet, making it obvious that we are about to leave. 'My,' I say, 'my husband isn't even in the ground, and you are trying to tarnish his name, you should be ashamed of yourself.'

'No, you should be, for not seeing what was happening in front of your nose, you are a stupid little girl,' her voice is raised, and she is now standing in front of me.

'The only stupid thing I have done is come here.'

I call the girls to tell them that we are leaving.

'You cannot run away from the truth Sarah,'

As if she thinks I am running away, I am walking out of this house before I do something I seriously regret.

'He was about to leave you, for me!' she smiles, 'He asked me to marry him, and we had a date planned and everything.'

She is fucking tapped in the head, 'Sharon he was married to me, now fuck off and stay away from us.'

'He is here with us now, ask the kids if you don't believe me, he is where he belongs, with me.'

Rachel is stood beside me.

'You are sick in the head,' I want to say a whole lot more, but that one line will do.

'Are you okay?' Rachel asks me.

'Yes, I am fine, come on love, let's get home.'

Sharon is still rambling on about how Stuart's ghost is with her daughters and how he keeps flicking her eldest daughter's hair, and that she knows it is Stuart because she can see him. I honestly think she is slightly deluded, so I tell Elise and Rachel to ignore her as we approach her front door. Sick twisted cow.

'He never loved you, you were just a cover story for us!' she is still shouting down the driveway at me when I turn and look at her.

'Sharon, these kids have been through enough heartache, without you adding to it, if there is any loving part of you in that black heart of yours, then I would suggest you keep well away from us all.'

I have just said that so calm and give myself a mental pat on the back. The girls look at me and smile, and I don't think they expected me to argue back with Sharon as they both knew that I was a little fearful of her, she is crazy after all.

Stuart didn't even like Sharon and had stopped talking to her altogether after she was very harsh and disrespectful to me one afternoon. He had warned her that I was his wife, and that no one would ever talk to me like shit. Only Stuart ever got away with being harsh with me and Sharon was put firmly in her place. Even Craig would have to sneak around to ours, without his bitch of a girlfriend knowing. This is the same woman who took almost three hundred pounds a week off Craig as soon as his wages were in the bank, she would then give him pocket money, for fuel or his lunches. Craig worked all the hours he could, so that Sharon could live the lifestyle she believed she deserved. She even claimed benefits for herself and the children and hid the fact that she and Craig have always lived together. The more I tell you about this woman, the more you will see why I am a hundred percent certain that Stuart would never have left me for her. He felt sorry for his best friend, even more so these past few years, Sharon sold her body to local men, I wouldn't know all the ins and outs, but I do know one of her clients got her pregnant and Sharon told Craig she was keeping the baby. She didn't keep it. Instead, she went and had an abortion, from what my Husband had told me, she was vile to Craig at the time, beating him up and that's when she started taking every penny off him. She knew her man was proud and wouldn't walk away from the kids, but she also knew that, if he had no money, then he was basically trapped there with her. Craig started to despise her and would tell Stuart just how bad things were getting, every time they had a secret visit. Stu even told Craig to come and stay with us for a while, but then Sharon threatened to have our house burnt down if he did.

Like I said, the more I tell you about her, the more you will see that she is the complete opposite to me, yet my husband was only with me because I reminded him of her? This still makes me laugh to this day.

On the walk home, the girls told me how Cathy and Sonya had told them the same bullshit story, which their mother had fed to me. Rachel said she laughed when Sonya told her, that they were meant to be step sisters.

'Apparently, Dad was going to marry Sharon this Christmas coming,' Elise sounds as entertained as me, 'She said Dad proposed to that psycho a few months back.'

'We know that is bullshit,' I say.

Apart from anything else, Stuart was that paranoid the past few months, that he spent every waking hour with me. If he wasn't with me, he always had one of the kids with him, and I really couldn't recall a time that he had gone up to see Craig this past year, so I know it was all lies. Doesn't stop you wondering though, does it?

MEETING THE MOTHER
IN LAW…

Malcolm and Judy got here just before midday, they dropped a few bits off at the house and made their way to the chapel of rest. I have been told to expect Stuart's Mum, Aunt, and brothers later today as Wendy had called Malcolm and told him that they were on their way. I am nervous about seeing Wendy for the first time, and I do wonder what she will make of me.

I have been married to her son for years and she has only ever seen a photo of me, from our wedding day. Stuart had invited his brothers, but his mother was told to stay away. At the time I tried to reason with Stu, but it turned into a large bicker, so I didn't push the matter.

It is the funeral tomorrow, and now that all the arrangements are in place, I am starting to worry. Firstly, because both of Stuart's parents are going to see their son in cut-off jeans and his favourite holey t-shirt. I am not sure they will understand that it was what their son wanted, they only have my word for it. Then there is the music as well.

Stuart told me who he wanted to be in charge of music, but Michael apologized and told us that he wasn't up to the job. Michael does at least know what song my husband wanted his coffin to be carried to and as much as the ones closest to Stuart will understand when they hear the soundtrack, I am worried how Wendy and Malcolm will take it.

Not much I can do about it now.

It feels like we have had visitors all day, which has been a good distraction for me at least. Carl has been out all day and has missed his Grandad when I called him to tell him that they were here, he just responded with, 'and what,' so you can guess what type of mood he is in today.

Elise is here keeping me company, and it is nice to spend some time with her. I taught Elise how to play the guitar last year, and she has improved since we last played together, she is better than me already, and I am so glad that her Dad talked her into learning.

It is Elise's birthday in a few months, and I at least know Stuart was hoping to buy her her own guitar. I don't mind her keeping my spare one, but I know it is a lot easier to learn on your own instrument.

'What do you want for your birthday?' I ask.

'The only thing I cannot have,' she says with tears in her eyes.

All I can do is take the guitar from her hand and wrap my arms around her, she starts to shake, her head buried in my hair.

I think this is the worst part of all of this. I can ignore my own pain, hell I have been used to hiding my emotions my whole life, so this isn't any different, but knowing that there is absolutely nothing I can do to ease the children's pain is a hard pill to swallow. Elise looks up at me with tear-drenched eyes.

'I am so glad Dad found you, Sarah, without you I am not sure any of us would be holding it together.'

'You call this holding it together?' I ask, with tears dripping off my chin.

'Yes, I do. You are the strongest person I know.'

'I don't feel strong Elise, not by a long shot,'

Just then the door-bell goes, it is twenty past three so must be Wendy and co. Elise answers the door for me, and I think she can sense my awkwardness. I have seen a photo of Wendy on Facebook when the big kids have spoken about her, and the odd time when Stuart wanted to Facebook creep her. Stuart was always dead against social media. He didn't mind the teenagers having it, but I was always forbidden. Even when we were advised to set up a business page. Stuart wouldn't agree.

Wendy looks the same as her profile picture and greets Elise and Lucy with a smile and hug. She has never met Lucy, but I was told the kids had sent her photos of both of my children last Christmas. Of course, Stuart didn't know as he would have gone through the roof.

'This must be my granddaughter,' Wendy says kneeling down to give Lucy a hug 'And what's your name?' she asks her.

Lucy just looks at me as if to ask if it is okay to talk to this woman in front of her, 'it's okay,' I reassure her.

'Lucy and this is Harry and Elise and my Mum.'

'She knows me,' Elise reminds Lucy while hugging her Nan who she hasn't seen in over six years.

Harry is hidden behind my legs and not wanting to talk, and he is quiet most of the time, so this is nothing new, I scoop him up into my arms and invite everyone in. It is nice to see Stuart's brother's; their friendly face puts me a little at ease as they start to talk about how it is strange seeing me without my baby bump. I was eight months pregnant when they last saw me.

We are in the living room when Carl walks in through the door, and I am a little worried as he did tell us this morning, that he was going to give his grandmother a piece of his mind. Carl is very loyal to his father, and now that Stuart is gone, he believes that he needs to take over his Dad's reins. Problem is, he seems to think these past few days, that he can get away with talking to me in the same abrupt manner that his Father used to talk to me when he was in a mood over something. I have let it slide for now, but after the funeral, I will need to sit him down and talk to him properly. For now, Debbie seems to be picking up the slack and trying to be a proper Mother to her son. Debbie is a very good Mum, but she and Carl have always clashed and that was the main reason that he came to stay with us in the first place.

As soon as he opens the front door, I am off my seat and walking towards the hallway. I was expecting him to still be in a bad mood, but instead, he puts his arm around me and tells me that he is sorry for being a dick lately. His Dad had just died six days ago, so I couldn't be angry with him, even if I tried.

After half an hour of chatting and getting to know each other, Michelle, Stuart's Aunt says that they need to think about going. The chapel of rest closes in just over an hour, and it will take them a good five minutes to drive there. Michelle seems kind enough, and even though she is my husband's Aunt, they are the same age. They grew up more like cousins. She has taken this harder than his own mother seems to, but I am assuming that she is very much like me and will hold her emotions in until she is on her own.

Three in the morning seems to be my crying time, every night this week I have cried myself to sleep, yet during the day, I am on autopilot and just get everything done in a state of numbness. I used to feel this numbness growing up, and it has me feeling sorry for myself.

We say our goodbyes and Wendy tells me that she will be here in the morning to help me any way she can. Stuart's funeral isn't till three in the afternoon, so I am hoping she doesn't turn up too early. With not falling to sleep until after three, I have been staying in bed till after nine, and I am hoping tomorrow is no different.

THE LONGEST GOODBYE...

As we get to the small chapel, I can see Malcolm talking to the woman who is doing our service. Jamie is with Rachel, so I make my way over to see them, and to make sure that Rachel remembered to bring the music. Malcolm has spotted me and made his way over to us. After sending Jamie into the chapel to prepare the music, Malcolm clears his throat.

'Can we all stand either side of the road please, they are about to turn into the drive,' his voice is loud and clear and reminds me of his son.

He says it is a drive, but the road must be at least two hundred feet long. Everyone moves into place, I am stood at the top of the line on the right-hand side, with all the kids around me. Standing opposite is Sharon, giving me the best bitch face glare she can.

I am not going to let this woman, make today any worse than it already is, so I just look away from her and avoid eye contact. As soon as the big black

39

hearse is in view, I am taken back when everyone starts clapping.

I would expect this for a well-known celebrity but wasn't expecting it for my Husband. Elise and Rachel both looked a little surprised too.

'Your Dad was clearly loved,' I say.

The clapping and cheers get louder as the vehicle comes to a stop. Craig, Michael, Daniel, and Carl all make their way over to the hearse, shortly followed by Malcolm and his brother Owen.

Seeing the six of them all forming a line to carry the coffin has me wondering how on earth they are going to get in through the chapel door. I smile to myself wondering if this was Stuart's plan in the first place. We have been visiting this place for years, so Stuart knew fine rightly that the doorway into the hall is tiny.

'Do you think they will get through the door?' Rachel asks me.

'I was just wondering the same thing,' we both smile at each other.

'Cue the music,' I smile.

Rachel and Elise look on at me nervously as I text Jamie and ask him to play the music. This first track is the most important and the one Stuart had picked out himself. The music starts, and I can feel a lot of eyes on me, well after all, it is the Simpson's theme tune. My Husband was a big kid at the best of times, but he reminded the kids and me of Homer Simpson, that character is so childish, and you really do end up feeling sorry for his wife Marge for putting up with everything that comes with marrying Homer. The same could have been said about me, but regardless of that, Stuart had picked this song, so it was being played no matter what.

The six men get the coffin through the door, but it was a very tight squeeze, and I hear Craig tell Malcolm; that they had almost dropped Stuart twice.

I smile at Craig as I walk past them and make my way to the church pew towards the front of the chapel. Sharon scowls at me but I don't look at her. Instead, I take my children's hands and lead them to our chairs. Lucy is looking all around her at all the faces she can recognize, there are a few who were invited by Stuart's friends, but everyone else here are the ones we call family, even if a few of them I have only met this week.

The service is short and sweet, and I am managing to keep it all inside as I feel the emotions rising inside me. I am in control until Craig gets up to say a few words. He starts by reading a short poem and then starts to talk about Stuart, and as he is talking, the tears are dripping down his face. Seeing this fully-grown man break down in front of us all, shows me that I don't need to remain strong for everyone else, I can cry too. As the service comes to an end and the music starts up again I can hear sobbing from every angle of the chapel, and that is it, I give in, and the tears silently stream down my face. Lucy hugs me as we stand up to follow the coffin outside. Rachel has been strong up to this point, as soon as the coffin is lowered into the ground, the poor girl breaks down. I think holding all that emotion in for this last week had really been taking its toll on her, and she is sobbing uncontrollably.

I am grateful that Debbie is here to help. As much as I want to walk over I check that my step daughter is okay, she has enough people fussing over her, and I have Harry getting very confused and clinging to my legs.

Debbie managed to book the pub at the end of the road for the wake, and I am glad because it means that everyone can come and join us. As we are walking down the road, I realize that we didn't arrange any food for the wake. Who has a wake without food? Us apparently.

I think I am the only person who seems to be annoyed about this, but it is my own fault, I did say at the start of the week, I would make food myself, to save on cost.

I still have no idea how much the chapel of rest is costing us, but Malcolm did say that we would have been charged extra with it being bank holiday weekend when his son passed away.

Like it was our fault or something. The last thing I should be stressing about is money, but I cannot help it.

I am so glad to get home finally, and as soon as I have Lucy and Harry settled in bed, I head to bed myself. Carl is staying out at Jack's house, and Rachel decided to stay with her Mum. Debbie has been really struggling today, and it has me feeling a little sorry for her Husband. She loved Stuart dearly and it has me wondering why I am not as cut up myself, after all, he was my husband, and he shared this bed with me for the past eight years. The bed always felt small; the way Stuart would sprawl across it every night. Now it feels massive and colder than normal.

I am sat here feeling completely sorry for myself and I am wondering what the hell I had ever done to deserve everything I have been through already. The worst of it is, no one believes me, and no one has ever wanted to believe me. Even my own family have always branded me a liar. Stuart wouldn't let me talk about my past and would tell me to ignore it ever happened. That was hard when he would tease me and say I was only so good at oral sex because I had been taught from such an early age.

I am angry, angry that he isn't here, and angry that I will never be able to tell him exactly what happened to me growing up, upset that he didn't even try to stay with us. Had Stuart listened to me instead of calling me a nag when I advised him to go to the hospital then he might still be here now, but he didn't, and I am left here all alone. I would have thought that my step children would have wanted to be here tonight with me, but I guess they are having an even harder time of it, after all, Stuart was their Father, and you only get one of them.

STEPPING INTO HIS
DAD'S SHOES...

It has been over a month now since Stuart passed away and we have all been getting on with life the best we can. It was Harry's birthday last week, and it was nice that Michael had arranged a small party for my son. He and Craig had both agreed that it would have been what his Daddy would have wanted. Stuart's friends never got involved before and didn't even send my kids cards, so the fact that they both have organized a street party has me beaming. That is until I see Sharon. Rumours are she has an aneurysm and is going to need an operation on her brain. I am unsure if I believe a word that comes out of her mouth, but everyone else seems to be falling for it. So much, so, that when I told Sarah about what Sharon had said to me the week my Husband died. She didn't seem surprised. I was told that the woman is ill, and to not let her get to me. In Sharon's eyes, that means that everyone believes her. I could scream at her and even scratch her eyes out, but instead I try to ignore her. That is a lot easier said than done when she keeps on with her wounded widow impression. I am sure it is making me look like a cold-hearted cow as well, but I know she is lying.

Even the big kids are sat in the garden talking to her, they have spent weeks slagging her off with me, but now that she apparently needs an operation on her brain, I am the bad guy.

Carl has been funny with me for the past few weeks, and at first, I put it down to him grieving, but he seems fine with everyone else and moody towards me. I am sure I haven't helped by working at the shop all the time, but I need to keep busy and Rachel has been happy enough to watch Lucy and Harry when they are not in school.

The shop has been stupidly quiet as well, no one knows what to say to me, and most of our regular customers are starting to avoid coming into the shop and heading to Tina's stall instead.

Tina is my rival, though I have always tried to be fair to her and try and stock different items to her.

She still won't try and get on with me. She hates the fact that I have managed to get hold of a lot of stock, cheaper than the average wholesale prices. I was lucky and bought out a gift shop in Kent when they were closing, so I managed to get hold of almost all stock retailing in the region of eleven grand for less than nine hundred, so even when Tina has a sale on, her prices are still higher than mine. Stuart and I were never that greedy, and he agreed with me when I said I would prefer to sell our stuff more affordably to gain returning customers. It worked, and within three months of being in the market, we had moved to a better more secure unit. This big unit that doesn't feel the same anymore. I am grateful to the few and far between customers who do come into the stall, but even then, I feel like I have a big 'wounded widow,' sign right across my forehead.

The good thing about the market being so quiet is that it has given me time to start up reading again. I have just started reading 'A child called it,' and wow, I thought I had it bad growing up. The poor boy in this book has been through hell and back and managed to come out the other side and become a well-known author. I could only imagine that happening for me.

It is the Bookman who pulls me from my trance as I am thinking about the book, which has got to me and makes me think about my own upbringing. He smiles at me, standing at the front of the till with his hands in his pockets.

'Well Sarah, have you been singing, it is starting to rain,' he jokes.

'I will have you know, I can sing actually.'

Well I say that, but I don't believe I can, I know I can hold a tune, but I wouldn't say beyond any means that I am a good singer, just not bad enough to make it rain.

'It is quiet today,' he says.

'Oh, I know, but it has been quiet for me for weeks,' I sigh.

'I have noticed that, do you think it is because of what happened?' he asks referring to Stuart.

'I did think that, but hey at least I have some peace to read,' I reply lifting the book I have almost finished.

Dave has always let me read his books, and he has that many of them crammed into his unit, I know he doesn't ever miss them.

'Tea?' I ask.

This is our little routine now, Dave will let me read as many books as I want and all he asks in return is one cup of tea a day. He refused to let me pay for the books and he knows I make a perfect cup of tea, so it is a win, win situation for both of us. I am just about the pass him his cup when he asks me if it is okay, for him to ask me something personal. For a second, I think he is flirting with me, and I feel somewhat uncomfortable.

'You have been through a lot,' he states, and now I am wondering where he is going with this.

'I don't just mean Stu either,' he thanks me for his tea and I let him continue to talk.

'Sarah, Stuart told me that you had it hard growing up,' he says.

I can't help but smile at the bookman, 'That is an understatement,' I joke.

'I am sorry to hear that, and it is none of my business, but I don't see why you don't write your own book,' he says.

I laugh at him, but he goes on to tell me that everyone has a book inside them and that it hasn't gone unnoticed the types of books I read.

'I wouldn't know where to start Dave, but it is worth a thought,' I smile thinking about my earlier thought process.

Dave takes his tea and walks back to his stall, he has a lady looking at one of his many book displays, but as soon as he gets close to his entrance to the bookstall, she walks away. That just makes me want to pay for this book I am about to finish reading.

I am starting to understand why everyone is bitching about how quiet it gets but in the same breath, we have Christmas coming up, and I know things will pick up then.

It is coming up to two o clock in the afternoon when my phone starts to ring, it is Rachel, and she has asked me if I can come home because Carl has come home in a stinking mood and taking it out on his big sister. I tell her that the market is dead anyway and hang up the phone. Dave sees me packing up and comes to asks me if everything is okay? I just tell him that the kids are acting up and that my family will always come first over a shop. I don't mean to sound rude, but I can tell I was a little irate as I left the market. I have a feeling that Carl and I are heading for a shouting match again tonight. He has been in a foul mood now for days, and it is starting to get beyond a joke. No one is liking being in the house when he is like this, and even with my brother staying with us full time and the fact that he is only twelve years older than Carl. He thinks as it was his Dad's house; that he has some hold over all of us. I was invited out by my cousin Katie the other day, and Carl had the cheek to tell me that I wasn't allowed to go out. That was a lovely evening of shouting, and I was just glad that Elise didn't stay over like initially planned. She gets upset when we all argue.

As soon as I walk towards the house, I can hear shouting, and this really is the last thing we need. I open the front door and Carl is stood over Rachel shouting about being woken up. I intervene, but I am rewarded with him spitting in my face and storming out of the front door, almost taking the door off its hinges.

I am shaking, and my blood is at boiling point, but I am unsure if it is fear or anger making me feel this way. Carl is at least a foot taller than me and towers above most of us; he even stood taller than his father. He and Stuart almost came to blows last year when Carl thought he would be a tough guy and go to swing at his Dad. Stuart realised that the situation could get out of control and managed to calm his son down without the use of violence. I wish he were here now to help with his son, but he isn't, and I don't think I have the energy to deal with all this added stress.

After talking to Rachel, I decide it is best to ring Debbie and ask if she minds having her son for a few days, just to give us all time to calm down. I am so angry that Carl spat in my face and I know if I see him again today I will explode. Part of me is glad Daniel is up visiting our Mother today. I think he would have slapped Carl, had he been here.

Debbie agrees to have her son and even comes up to ask if Rachel will go home as well. I am grateful when she declines the offer, saying that she would prefer to stay with me instead.

'I couldn't leave you on your own,' she says as soon as her Mum has gone.

'I wouldn't have minded,' I say, but I think I would have been a little upset if she had left.

Rachel and I have started to become close lately, and I am glad that she is now a little older, and we can have more grown-up conversations, in saying that, she has always been wise beyond her years, but now that she is turning eighteen I feel I can be more open with her. We are sat in my bedroom just talking about random stuff when I tell her that I am thinking about writing a book.

'I will never publish it,' I say, 'it is just my way of getting it out of my head and onto paper,'

'What will you write about?' she asks.

'I think I am going to write a book about my childhood,' I explain.

'Oh, Dad did say that you had it really bad growing up and that your Dad used to beat you up,' she gives me a saddened look.

'Trust me, he did a lot more than that, but that is a story I would rather write than talk about,'

I want to tell her everything, but I promised Stuart that I wouldn't ever tell his kids too much about my past.

Stuart never knew the whole story himself, so I feel awkward just thinking about telling his eldest daughter.

That and the fact that no one has ever believed me in the past, I think part of me, still has that expectation with everyone I have ever almost told.

'I think you should write, especially if it helps you,' Rachel holds my hand and squeezes it slightly 'Do you want a coffee?' she asks.

'Thank you, sweetheart.'

It is a few days later when Carl finally shows his face. He tells me that he was having a bad day and that he is sorry. He then goes on to say that he has had a boring time back at his Mother's house and asked me if he can move back in. Of course, I agree, I would never turn one of these kids away unless I really needed to.

For a few days' things really calm down in the house, Carl has been helping more with the kids, mainly Harry, taking him to the shop with him and going to the park. It is Harry's birthday in a few days and I have been told not to worry about a party because Stuart's friends want to arrange it for me and that Claire has made a cake already for him.

I have only met Claire a few times, but she seems nice enough. She is the girlfriend of Michael's eldest son, and she was also Lucy's nursery school assistant, so Lucy likes her.

I have got Harry a Nintendo DS because that is all he has asked for since last Christmas and apart from getting him a few small bits to open as well on the day, his birthday hasn't been much stress this year. I feel bad that we will be having a party just weeks after the death of his Dad, but what can I do? Harry deserves to be happy, and that is all that matters at the end of the day.

Carl is in town and has just rung me up to ask me what size shoe his little brother is in, so I am guessing he is buying shoes for Harry. Not that he needs them, my son has more pairs of shoes than me and his sister put together.

The party is a bunch of chairs placed outside Michael's house with music faintly playing through the kitchen window, but I am just grateful that everyone is here, and we are all celebrating together. Unfortunately, my Mum can't make it, but everyone else is here. Harry seems happy enough and Lucy is in her element with all the girls. The mood soon changes when Craig pulls up with his and Sharon's kids, and then she walks out of the car. The woman had the cheek to invite herself by the looks of things and I am not impressed but I don't want to cause a scene. I do my very best to ignore the woman completely, but I am feeling very jealous when all of Stuart's kids are sat around her, laughing and joking with her and her kids. I wouldn't mind, but they know the lies she was telling because she told them too, so how they can be okay with her I will never know. It is almost six in the evening, and Harry gets settled for bed at seven, so

I make my excuses and leave. We have been here for over three hours, so it isn't as if I am eating and leaving. Rachel comes home with the kids and me, but Carl and Elise stay with Sharon and Craig, and I don't even think Carl noticed us leaving.

Lucy and Harry were knackered as I put them to bed and Rachel and I are just watching the TV. I couldn't tell you what was playing because I am too deep in thought. Just then my old best friend Mona messages me on Facebook. I have only been on here a week and not had a chance to get to grips with the app. I am excited when she invites me out with her that weekend.

When Stuart was alive, I was told that I am never allowed on social media, and now that I am, the guilt is starting to get to me. Rachel says that I am silly and that the whole world has Facebook, so I shouldn't feel bad, but I do. We only signed me up to Facebook so that I could create a tribute page for Stuart, so his friends could leave a message for him, but reading through all the comments has me feeling a little sadder than I have done for the past few weeks. People I do not know or haven't even met are commenting on his photo. My jealousy takes over when I woman comments to say that Stuart was the nicest man she had ever met.

'Do you know her?' I ask Rachel who is sat beside me on the sofa.

'I'm not sure, search her mutual friends,' she says.

'Mutual friends?' I don't even know how to do that.

'Here I will show you.'

Rachel takes my phone and is like a private detective the way she is scrolling through this woman's feed.

'Nope, we don't know her, but you get this sometimes,' she says.

'I mean your profile pictures are public so that anyone can like or comment, unfortunately.'

'Oh, fair enough, by the way, my old best mate has asked if I want to join her on a night out,' I say to judge Rachel's response.

'You really should go Sarah,' she smiles.

'I will think about it, although I think you should come with me,' I say.

Rachel jumps at the chance and in all honesty, I think I would feel a lot better with Rachel with me. I cannot remember the last time I was out. Stuart and I went out a few times at the very start of our relationship, but we didn't have a night out in at least eight years; so, I wouldn't know where to begin.

'She is on about this weekend if we are up to it.'

'Yes, we are,' Rachel announces as she gets up to her feet.

'Smoke time?' she asks.

So, we are both in the garden, the two little ones are fast asleep upstairs, and for a second, I had forgotten that Carl was due in. I hear him shout my name as he makes his way through the house.

'You will wake the kids up,' I hiss as he comes into my view.

Carl seems in a good enough mood, and we are just chatting in the back garden when Rachel tells Carl that we need him to babysit for the weekend.

'Why?' he asks.

'So that me and Sarah can have a night out.'

'Oh, fair enough, who with?' he asks.

By this point I have walked into the kitchen to make a fresh coffee, when I hear Carl, asking lots of questions; like who the hell is Mona, and did she think Dad would have let me go out.

Well I know the answer to that, I know for a fact that if Stuart were here, he wouldn't want me going out at all, but the fact that I am taking Rachel with me, I think proves somehow that I am not doing it to spite their father. I deserve a night out more than most, and I am looking forward to it. I message Mona and ask if it is okay to bring a friend and that I am looking forward to a well needed night out. Mona knows what we have been through this past few weeks so was keen for me to agree to the night planned.

'That's is all sorted,' I say to Rachel as I walk back into the garden holding three cups of coffee.

'I didn't want one,' Carl says getting to his feet.

'Not to worry, more for me,' I joke, but Carl isn't looking in a joking mood as he snarls back at me.

'I will be in my room!' he snaps.

'What's up with him?' I ask, but Rachel just shrugs her shoulders.

We don't see Carl till almost six in the evening the next day, I was at the market all day, and Rachel refused to wake her brother up, and I really cannot blame her, he is a nightmare lately.

I decide to take Harry and Lucy with me shopping that evening while Rachel and myself go and get an outfit for the following evening. I am so excited that I feel sick, or maybe that is nerves.

CARL, HOW COULD YOU?!

It is an hour before we are due to meet Mona and I am starting to stress, it has been over five years since I have even tried to apply my make-up and as I am painting my face, I am starting to remember how much hard work it is.

I stopped wearing make-up after Stuart and I had been together for a while, he hated the fact that it makes me look so young, but being thirty now, I am hoping to look younger. It was different before. I had to put my Husband's feelings first, with him being a lot older than me, because he used to worry that he would look like a paedophile with his tiny young wife by his side.

That conversation stuck with me, and the last thing I wanted was for him to feel like he looked like a sick twisted man like my own Father, so I stopped wearing make-up. Stuart would tell me that I looked beautiful without it, and at first, I didn't believe him, but as the years went on, I started to get used to my natural look. Today though, I want to look different, I want to feel pretty.

I have used Rachel's straighteners, and I am shocked at how long my hair is, I always have my hair tied up, or I have it braided down the right-hand side and normally because of having the kids and running the market. I cannot remember the last time I spent this long getting ready. Rachel walks into my bedroom.

'Wow, Sarah, you look so different; look at your hair!' she gasps as she starts running her fingers down my waist length hair.

'I know I didn't realise it was so long.'

'Honestly Sarah, it looks like you have had extensions put in, and it is so soft.'

Rachel spends the next few minutes playing with my hair as I finish applying the last of my make-up. I do look so different, but I love my reflection today.

Carl walks into my bedroom followed by Lucy.

'Mummy you look so pretty,' Lucy says smiling at me.

'Yeah a little too pretty if you ask me,' Carl sounds snappy.

'Come on mate, how can anyone look too pretty?' I smile at him, but he snaps back.

'Do you really think I am going to let you go out looking like that?!'

What the hell, who does he think he is talking to? I am his stepmother and he needs to remember that.

'I am sorry, Carl, but I don't see how it has anything to do with you,' I say as calmly as I can.

'You can't speak to her like that!' Rachel snaps.

'I can, and I will, my Dad has been dead for five minutes, and you are dolling yourself up like a slapper!'

Oh, I am ready to smack this cheeky little shit, but I bite my tongue.

'Dad didn't let you wear makeup and the first chance you have, you are wearing a shit ton of it,' he says all matter of a fact.

'I am not being funny Carl,' I pause and take in a deep breath, 'Your father is no longer here, and I know it hurts mate, but don't you dare talk to me like this.'

I can feel myself welling up, so I take another deep breath, 'I will wear and look how the hell I want to!'

'Not if I have something to do with it,' he states as cold as ever.

'And what do you mean by that?' I ask, but he just looks at his sister who is now sat on her Dad's side of the bed.

'Mummy looks nice,' Lucy says pulling Carl's arm to go and play with her again on the Play-Station. 'Come and play,' she says pulling on his arm.

'Not now!' he snaps.

'Hey, if this is the way you are going to be with us again Carl, then I suggest you leave.'

'No, what so you can get a man home, in my father's bed?!' he shouts.

'Right that is enough, you are just plain nasty now!' Rachel gets to her feet, 'Sarah has been through so much and is entitled to let her hair down, it is nothing all to do with you!'

I haven't seen her get so annoyed and I am grateful that she is backing my corner. I put make-up on this evening to make myself look and feel better, and Carl has walked in and made me feel worse than his Dad ever did, just because I wanted to feel a little better. I cannot live like this and seeing how Carl is acting over it is making me realise just how controlling his Dad was. Stuart, I think had a gentler approach to it all, but like Carl just said; his Dad never 'let me' wear make-up or at least that is how it must have looked to Stuart's kids. Was I really that controlled? Either way, I cannot let a seventeen-year-old boy think he can tell me what to do in my own home.

'Carl, please leave. I am going out tonight whether you like it or not'

'Well I am not babysitting,' he says as he walks out of the room.

'That's okay, I didn't ask you to, for your information, Daniel will be here any minute.'

I haven't even asked my brother yet, but I am sure he will be happy enough to watch the kids for me, I know he is just sat in the house playing the computer and he will be grateful for the extra few quid in his pocket. It is a few minutes later when I hear the front door slam. I walk over to the bedroom window knowing that Carl will walk towards the carpark out the back; it is the only way to walk from ours to his mate Jack's house and Jack is the only person who can put up with Carl's mood swings.

Jack's own Father passed away suddenly a few years ago so, he can relate to what his best friend is going through, but even Jack has had a few words with Carl these past few weeks for the way he is treating everyone.

Daniel gets here just as the taxi pulls up out the back, and I have enough time to tell him that I have put the oven on for his pizza and have left a few beers in the fridge before Rachel is dragging me out of the house.

'Call me if you need me,' I shout just as my brother closes the back door.

As much as I am trying my hardest to enjoy tonight, I just cannot relax. Arguing with a teenage boy is not the best way to start a Saturday evening, and I am too tired even to get up to sing on karaoke; which isn't like me at all. It is nice catching up with Mona though I do see how much we have changed over the years.

My friend seems very confident and has almost every part of her body out on show. I guess if you have it, you should flaunt it, but I have had a face full of boob or bum all night.

She seems louder now as well, which must be part of this new-found confidence. I on the other hand, seem very shy compared to the Sarah she used to know.

Listening to her talk about the past ten years that we haven't seen each other has me thinking that I am glad I was blissfully married and haven't really had much drama. Mona has been through so much, that I could write a book about her. It is nice to hear that she has sorted herself out and got off all the drugs; that was the main reason I distanced myself from her, I had just had children and Mona was out partying and taking every drug handed to her. I used to say that at least she had that partying experience. I had always wanted to know what it was like, obviously minus the drug taking.

I keep clock watching, and as soon as it hit ten thirty I am looking for Rachel to ask if she is ready to go home, I feel bad when I find her throwing up in the girl's loos.

I was so wrapped up in catching up with my old best friend that I didn't even notice Rachel leave our table.

We get home with no accidents in the taxi. Although I did ask the driver to take a detour to the cash machine because I was convinced that Rachel would leave me with an eighty-pound cleaning fine, but luckily, she is fine until we get back indoors.

I am glad that Carl spends the whole evening in his room and my brother is already asleep so as soon as I know Rachel is okay, I make my way to bed myself. I haven't enjoyed myself this evening, and I am feeling deflated as I sit down on my bed, with more force than is needed. I don't turn the light off to start with. I just stare at myself in the mirror, I am only half looking and more gazing into thin air.

I am soon startled when I think I see a shadow behind me.

It was probably just my eyes adjusting, but I do wonder if it is Stuart's spirit watching over us, and then I am reminded of Sharon's comment about how his ghost is always in her home, where he belonged. I fall asleep while gently crying to myself.

A few days later when Carl and myself come to a real standstill. He is snappy and moody as usual, but this morning he stormed out of the house over being woken up before midday. I was at the market and had a phone call from Elise who had popped in to see her sister.

Rachel was still in bed, and Lucy and Harry were basically looking after themselves. It was agreed the night before, that

Carl would get up with the kids and let Rachel have a lie in, after all, she had been up every morning with them for the past few weeks. We caught Carl in a good mood and it was agreed. This morning when I woke him, he was fine, but from what Elise has just told me on the phone, he got annoyed when she turned up saying that he couldn't sneak back to bed if she were at the house.

'I told him it made more sense if he went to bed while I was there, but he just bitched at me,' Elise sighs down the phone.

'Where are you and kids now?' I ask.

'We are still at yours, Rachel is awake now but not being very helpful.'

'Do you need me to pack up shop and come home?' I ask.

Packing up early seems to become a routine this past month, and I am starting to realize I cannot rely on the big kids to watch my two. It isn't fair on them.

'No, we will be fine for a few hours,'

After an hour or worrying, and with the market being quiet, I decided to close early anyway. I know Elise said that they would be fine until I got home, but I really could do with being there when Carl turns up. I empty the till which I do every Saturday and start to bring some of the tables in from the front of my unit.

'You are leaving early again?' I hear a deep male voice behind me.

'Yes, sorry Kay, kids again.'

Kay is the market management and has already been on at me lately about packing up early, but in all honesty, I don't care what he has to say, what is the worst that will happen? He might tell me I have to give up my unit, but I am starting to wonder if that is such a bad idea.

I have lost every inch of passion and soul in this place anyway, and I really am starting to think about selling up, not that the big kids will let me, they have talked me into adding, 'In loving memory,' onto the business cards which I was fine with. Although I never hand them out anymore. Like I said before; I already feel like I have a wounded widow sign above my head.

The house is calm when I get in, and Rachel is surprised to see me at half past one in the afternoon.

'Why are you home?' she asks.

'Because I missed you,' I joke 'The market was dead anyway.'

'Seriously, on a Saturday?'

'I know love; it is getting worse.'

I am only home forty minutes when Carl comes in the back garden with Jack, looks like he has another new bike. I have asked him where he is getting all this new stuff, and how he is funding his weed habit, but I just get told that he has been swapping shit, for good stuff. I don't mean to cause an argument as soon as he walks in through the door, but I have to ask how much his latest bike set him back because it is looking brand new.

'I swapped it for my old BMX,' he states, but I don't believe him.

We bicker for a few moments, and then he goes up the stairs, Jack following behind him.

Elise has asked if she can stay over, which she knows she never has to ask me, and she reminds me that it is the X factor semi-finals tonight. We agree that I need to go and get some crisps and popcorn for later and she offers to take Lucy for a walk with her to the shop. Rachel decides to take a walk as well with Harry which means I can get five minutes on my own.

Just as the kids walk out the front door, Carl and Jack come down the stairs again. They are only in the kitchen a few minutes and then leave themselves.

The house is eerily silent. I take my handbag up to my bedroom so that I can transfer the week's shop takings into my saving pot. Initially, Stuart and I were saving for a family holiday, but now the jar has a label titled headstone fund on it instead. Looking online it is going to cost us at least three grand for a nice enough headstone, and I have at least eight hundred in here just in notes.

The pot is sealed both sides so when it is time to take it to the bank, which feeling the weight of this, will not be too far away. We will have to get a tin opener to it.

I have already purchased another money box to replace this one. I have just added another two hundred to the pot, so we are a third of the way there already, and I only started saving a few weeks ago.

I have only just finished paying off my funeral bill, and that set me back, more than this headstone is going to.

I look at myself in the mirror and can see how drained I am looking. Do you know what, I am going to put a bit of make-up on and do my hair again! I felt good about myself last weekend and pretty for the first time in years.

I think the girls are taking their time on purpose, but I am not complaining, by the time they get back, I have cleaned up and prepared the dinner.

'You look really nice Sarah,' Elise smiles at me. 'Make-up makes a difference.'

'I told you,' Rachel says flicking my straightened hair.

'Sarah, you should make an effort more often, you are beautiful,' Elise hugs me.

I start serving up dinner, which Rachel texts her brother to tell him his food is ready, she gets a reply tell her that he has already eaten at Jacks, so we sit down and eat our food. I decided on a chicken Balti tonight, and it is X factor after all. We have fudge cake for dessert. My favourite.

I head up to bed at just gone one in the morning, Daniel is in Carl's room next door playing on his Xbox, but Carl is nowhere to be seen. I thought he would have at least sent a message to say that he is staying out, and I don't even know if he has his key, so I can't lock the front door. I say my goodnights and close my bedroom door over, I am not sleepy but have decided to start a bit of writing and just see if it helps me.

Since Harry and the kids have lost their Father, it has me thinking of the man who produced me. I am sure my own Dad is off having a wonderful life, while I just seem to have drama, after drama. It makes me angry that he is always the one who comes out on top, and I am left here like a wounded child. No more, I say to myself as I start to type the words in my brain onto my computer screen. It's almost four in the morning before I decide I need sleep.

Sunday morning has evaded me, and the others must have left me in bed because when I look over at the clock, it is just gone midday. I am frustrated because I wanted to get up early, but I think I needed that sleep. Is it bad that I want to hide up here all day? I open my bedroom door, and I can hear Carl and Daniel talking in the kitchen, I can't make out what is being said, but Carl laughs which has me thinking he is in a good enough mood.

As soon as I walk down the stairs, I get a comment off Carl about me being a lazy bitch, and I snap back at him. I tried to hold it in for a whole second before I snap back.

'That is rich coming from you.'

I wish I had kept that thought in my head because it seemed like that was the starting point to our day. Carl was purposely trying to wind me up, bitchy comments and snarky remarks at every given opportunity and my patience was wearing thin. By three in the afternoon, we had a blazing row over how he seems to have a lot of money lately, he said I was accusing him of stealing, but I wasn't. I was just trying to find out the truth. We were both screaming at each other when Rachel and Daniel decide to leave us to it and get the kids out of the house for a while.

Carl was relentless and not backing down, but I was getting more and more irate with each word that escaped his lips. Finally, he stormed out of the house but not before backing me into a corner and screaming in my face that I was nothing but a gold digging slag. That seems funny now when I think back, as I was the primary earner in our family and it was my gift shop that gave Carl all his pocket money. I just smile slightly, as he walks closer to me, his hot wet breath against my cheek and he whispered in my ear.

'Don't forget Sarah, you haven't got my Dad to protect you now,' he hissed before walking out of the front door.

I can hear him shouting outside, but I am numb and just walk into the kitchen as if nothing had happened. I honestly thought that he was about to hit me, our doors in the house show his signs of rage already and part of me has been waiting for the day he tried to raise his hand at me. Then I see my Mum walk through the front door.

'What was all that about?' she asks.

I explain that he has been in this foul mood for weeks now and that it is clear he hates me at the minute.

'What have you done?' she asks.

Like why did I have to do something to get given abuse? But I don't say that instead I just look at her.

'Being alive.'

'Oh, Sarah you don't need to put up with it, tell his mother to take him back.'

I know my Mum is right but how can I kick a six-teen-year-old boy out, just months after his father has died? Yes, he can go to his mother and stay with them, so it isn't as if I am making him home-less, but I still wouldn't know if I could do it.

'You need to start thinking about yourself Sarah, and if not those kids,'

I put the kettle on to make us a drink, but also so I can turn my face away from her and fight back the tears.

'He was just shouting at me when I walked in,' she says.

I turn to look at my Mum to ask what was said because all I could hear was shouting.

'He said that you needed a good seeing to, that you are lucky he hasn't washed the floor with you, Sarah I am worried he will hit you,' I can tell my Mother is concerned in her tone of voice.

'Honestly Sarah, you will not forgive yourself if he lashes out at the kids,'

She's right and when she leaves half an hour later, I find myself sitting on the floor in my bedroom and just staring into thin air. My mind is going crazy, with all the what if's.

That evening after Carl has had a smoke and calmed down, I attempt to talk to him calmly, and I explain that I thought he was going to hit me, I think I offended him slightly, but I had to be honest.

'I know I cannot act that way in front of the kids, but you frustrate me,' he says.

I am trying not to say anything when he starts to mimic his Father's tone of voice and lovely use of words.

'Sometimes I think you forget I am the adult here,' I state.

'Really, then start fucking acting like one, you bring shame to our family.'

'Where the fuck did that come from?' I snap.

'Yeah bro, that is totally uncalled for,' my brother steps in. 'Sarah has done nothing but support you, even when you are being a little shit.'

'Who stopped you getting kicked out of school?

Who took you in when your Mother said she couldn't cope?' I ask.

'My Dad did,' he smirks at me.

Stuart really didn't want Carl with us at the start, and our house was a relaxing environment considering we had two young children and the thought of having his teenage son living with us, not long after Harry was born, was a scary thought for my Husband.

I was the one who talked him into giving his son a chance. I owned my own guilt over my son Mark, so I was rather forceful with the subject, and as for Carl's schooling.

If it weren't for all those meetings and constant talks with different schools, Carl would never have received an education. It wasn't ideal, but he did leave school well on his way to be a qualified motorbike mechanic, and none of that would have happened without me pushing for it. I remind Carl of all of this, and he just sits and rolls his eyes at me.

It is taking all my strength not to throw him out of my house, and I am sick to the back teeth of all the arguing, so I tell my brother than I am off to bed. I do invite Daniel to come and chill in my bedroom with me and have a smoke with his big sister, but he says he is knackered himself so is planning an early night.

It all finally come to a head a few days later. I have been adding money to a metal money box for over three months now, and I know that we must be close to the three-grand target we want for Stuart's headstone.

Carl had been keen to tell me not to open the money box, he is adamant that we need to wait until the thing is full, but I explain that we have another tin waiting and that I am going to the bank in the morning anyway.

'You need to wait till it is full, will only take you about a week, maybe two,' he says.

'You know what I am like,' I joke 'When I get something in my head I stick to it,' and I do.

'Yeah Carl, don't you want to know how much we have saved?' Rachel asks her brother.

'Yeah, but a few weeks won't make much difference,' he says before telling us that he is heading out for the day.

'Where are you heading?' I ask.

I ask him this question every time he plans to go out, and normally he would happily tell me and his Dad what his plans for the day were, but Carl just looks at me and tells me that it is his business and that I don't need to know where he is going or who he is with.

'Must be a girl,' Rachel says as her brother makes his way down the stairs. I cannot help but give her a big smile.

'Do you want me to get the tin opener?' she asks, getting to her feet.

'Yes, please sweetheart.'

I attach the tin opener to the top of the oversized metal can, and push down to pierce the metal, the satisfaction is written all over my face, I give the opener a few turns before asking Rachel if she would like to open the rest. She is excited as she takes it from me.

'I am guessing we have at least five hundred in here,' she smiles.

'We should have a lot more than that,' I explain 'I put over eight hundred in there the first few weeks, and everyone else has been adding change and the odd note into it too.'

'Wow then well over a grand!' she says excitedly 'we will be able to get Dad's headstone before his anniversary for sure.'

'That will be nice,'

The tin is open, and the money comes rushing out onto the bed, but the notes have stayed inside the tin.

Rachel starts to pull the notes out, but it is clear by her face there is a problem. The money is short and not by a little bit either, the only notes that are still in the tin are the few that I put in there myself last night. Instead of eight hundred pounds like I remember one hundred percent putting in there, we have four twenty-pound notes folded into a square. All the other notes have disappeared.

'I thought these tins couldn't be opened without a tin opener?'

I am shocked and annoyed as it looks like someone has stolen Stuart's money. Who the fuck would steal money from a dead man? It is bad, but I am wondering if Carl may have something to do with it, and if not, I think he knows who did. Why else would he be so sure that opening the tin was a stupid idea, and that I should wait? I am hoping he had just decided to use the money for something and was thinking he could replace it before it was needed.

'Are you thinking what I am thinking? Rachel asks.

'What are you thinking?'

'I don't want to sound like a bitch, but Carl has been flashing the cash lately, do you think it could be him?'

'Maybe, but even if it isn't him, I do think it is one of his mates,' I say.

'What about your brother?'

'Daniel?' I ask.

Daniel is the only brother that I talk to lately, so I know that is who she means, and in all honesty, I hadn't thought about him until now. He has always been a bit of a bad boy, and he has been known to use his five-finger discount from time to time, but I would like to think he has never stolen from me. Stuart and Daniel were very close, but of course so was Carl and his Dad.

'I don't want to think it is anyone we know, but it must be,' I say.

Carl is out most of the evening and when he returns he has a new pair of beats headphones. They retail at about sixty pounds at least so as you can imagine, I questioned him when he hands them over to his younger sister Elise, telling her that they are a late Christmas present.

'Where did you get the money for them?' I ask.

'Not that it is any of your business, but I swapped them,' he snaps.

I don't try to hide my disbelief when he starts telling me his story about how his mate hated the headphones, so wanted to swap for a pair of three-pound headphones that I had bought for Carl a few weeks previous.

'You cannot blame me for asking,' I say.

'Who else have you accused?' he asks.

'My brother and I will be asking anyone else who has been in the house over the last few months, but Carl you haven't done any favours by telling us not to open the tin,' I snap.

'It was like you knew that the money would be short,' Elise said, who has been filled in on the day's events.

'I even got asked dude,' Daniel pipes up from the kitchen where he is making us all a drink.

'Do you know what, I am not standing for this,' Carl gets up to his feet and walks towards me.

'You are a sick fuck up, and I wish you were laying in that ground, not him.'

Carl is pointing to the photo of his Dad on the fireplace.

'You really think I would take off my own father?' his voice is deep and scares me with his calm tone.

That has me glad that everyone is here otherwise I know he would have slapped me. I cannot keep living like this, worried I could receive a slap if I try and ask a question or need to put my foot down. Carl honestly acts like he is the adult, and I am the child who needs to be taught a lesson.

'I can't do this anymore,' I say.

'Mum did say he could go back to hers,' Elise informs me.

'Hey, but he has said he wouldn't leave,' Rachel responded.

'Oh, I don't know what to think anymore,' and I really don't. My head is a mess lately.

I NEED TO MOVE ON…

It has been almost eight months since Stuart passed away and I have been thinking for a while that I cannot keep going on like this, I feel numb. The big kids don't help around the house, and even Rachel has started to frustrate me by refusing to get out of bed while I go to the market, all I have asked, is if one of them can get up and collect my kids from school at three in the afternoon but I have had to leave the market early most days because I haven't been able to get through to the teenagers, to make sure they are awake. I am probably overthinking, but the last thing I need is the school to ring social services if my kids are always being picked up late.

I decide a few nights up at my Mother's house is the best thing I can do, and as for the market, well that can stay closed for a few days. It isn't as if I am missing much anyway because it is always quiet in the winter. I had a few good weeks in the run-up to Christmas which meant we were finally able to pay for the headstone, but I had learned my lesson and saved the money myself in a bank account.

Mum seems happy to see me, and we spend most of the afternoon chatting and bitching about the past few weeks. I explain that the big kids are causing me more stress than the two little ones and my Mum tells me that I should get my house back.

'I can't just kick them both out!' I explain.

'And why not? I am not being funny, but they have a mother down the road from you.'

'I know, and Debbie has tried to get Carl to go home, but he refuses,' I say.

'How are things between you and him now?' she asks.

'Oh, nothing has changed,' I say, 'we don't talk to each other and to be honest, I try my hardest to avoid him. I spend most of the time in my bedroom writing now.'

'Oh, you did say, what are you writing?' she asks.

For the first time since I started escaping into my writing, I am feeling bad, and I hadn't thought about anyone else involved in my past. Now I think I am feeling I ping of guilt as I tell my Mum that I am writing about my childhood.

'Oh,' is all she says.

I know my Mum has never really believed me, she thinks that my Dad's version of events is how it all happened, but I cannot talk to her about it, the last time I tried was too hard for me, and the repercussions were not worth any of it. She tells me to my face that she knows I am telling the truth but then I hear that she has told everyone else that I am a liar. Even though I know all this, I just let her think that I believe that she knows what I say is true, but I am far from stupid.

It was a few years ago when I realized that I was being talked about behind my back. I had made the mistake of getting totally off my face, and telling my cousin Jody all about my past, again. She told me that she wanted to believe me but that when she asked my Mother, she was told that I had made the whole thing up. I was upset beyond words because my Mum was the only person who saw what he was like and that even though she didn't see the sexual abuse, she saw enough shit to know that the man was a monster, yet she was still defending him.

I know her and my Father talk on the phone from time to time as I still get reminded now and again, when she has a conversation with me about the man.

I suppose it was always normalized for us and that's why she finds it so easy to pretend that none of it happened. I think part of me is hoping that she will read my book one day and realize what I did go through, but I somehow doubt it.

We have been drinking cheap vodka mix drinks most of the evening, but I am feeling slightly drunk already.

I tell my Mum that I think I need to call it a night and make my way up the stairs to share a bed with my son. It feels awkward and a little weird feeling someone in bed with me, even if it is only my six-year-old son, I have been sleeping on my own for so long now.

The next morning, I wake with such a sore head, the vodka didn't sit well with me. I am grateful when Mum offers me a bacon sandwich and hands me a coffee.

'I am never drinking again,' I moan but my Mum just laughs at me.

My mother and I sit in the kitchen while my son goes off to play with my younger brother and sister. Mum then reminds me that I told her that I want to get away for a while.

'I was drunk, so it must be the truth,' I joke but it wasn't a joke at all, and I did want to get away, I just worried too much about what other people would think.

Mum then goes on to tell me that she has been thinking about going back to Ireland herself and tells me I should think about whether I would ever end up going over to stay with her once she is set-tled. I have thought about moving away, and it seems more appealing the more she talks about where she used to live. I know my Mother only stayed here because Stuart died, and she had al-ways planned to go back at some point, I just don't think I expected it so soon.

'Are you thinking like real soon, or in the future?'

I ask concerned that I am about to lose her again.

I really should be used to it by now; my Mother never stays in one place too long, she always moves back here for a year or so, and then moves away again. She was living in Cornwall for a brief time, and I regret not visiting her while I had the chance.

'I don't know how soon, but I know I hate it here,' she says, and I must agree with her.

This is the estate that I lived in as a young girl, and it doesn't hold many good memories for me at all. The whole of this depressing town makes me feel down when I start to think about it.

What do I really have left here?

If you had asked me a few months ago if I would ever consider moving away and leaving the big kids behind, back then I would have felt almost offended but the way my life seems to be spiralling out of control, I am wondering what to do.

It has been over a week since I had a lengthy conversation with my Mum about moving away and with me being on Facebook now and in touch with some of my friends over in Ireland, I am thinking even more about my situation.

Rachel has been quiet lately and spent a lot of the time either down at her boyfriend's house or in bed, so we don't see much of each other. It isn't like it was a few months ago, and I am guessing the constant stress with her brother has led to most of this.

Carl has been on ultimate wind up mode lately, and it feels like he is doing everything he can to cause added stress. Whether it is throwing an open bag of peas in Rachel's bed at three in the morning and creating a massive scene, causing the small children to think it was time to be awake to him filling the kids up with sweets and making them hyper, knowing that I have been running the shop all day.

Whereas Elise and I have bonded lately, I teach her the guitar, and for her birthday I went out and bought her a beautiful guitar in its own case.

I had told her that me and her Father had seen it a few months before he passed and that he said he was getting it for her. Which was true, but Stuart had told me at the time, that he wasn't willing to spend so much on his daughter when she was still so young. I had seen how naturally she picked up the guitar and she made it easy to be her teacher. I think Elise is the one who I will miss the most.

I have talked myself into leaving, telling myself that it is the best thing for the children, and myself.

It was a trip to the doctors and being told that I have lost almost two stone in a matter of months that really made it hit home for me. I am skinny anyway and very small in height, so I couldn't afford to lose two stone. My doctor has advised me to take these crazy tablets that sedate you and force you to sleep but most importantly, they would give me a massive appetite. I cannot swallow tablets anyway, but I still agreed and took the prescription to the chemist.

Once I got home, I read through the information leaflet that came with my large tablets. There was no way on this earth I could have digested these things, not just due to their size, but also because the side effects scared the shit out of me. Most common where things like sickness and head aches, no thank you. The little less common where hallucinations and vivid dreams.

'They sound like funky arse pills,' my brother Daniel says as I am reading the side effects out to him.

'Sound like LSD if you ask me,' I joke.

There is no way I will take them so when Daniel asks if he can try them out, I let him. My brother has always dabbled in drugs, nothing too hard-core, but was happy to try my anti-depressants.

The next day he tells me that he is glad I never took the tablets myself.

'Did you enjoy them that much?' I joke.

'Nah, they were bizarre,' he confesses, 'I really needed a pee and couldn't move, I couldn't even lift my head to get up.'

I am trying my hardest not to laugh at him, 'Did you piss yourself?'

'No, but it was a close call.'

I tell my brother how I am going over to Ireland with our Mother and that I need to get away from everything for a while.

'I agree with you sis, you need to think of yourself for a change,' he smiles at me, but I know he will miss me as much as I will miss him, 'But wait a minute, Mum hasn't told me she is moving back, when did she decide this?'

My brother gets on the phone with my Mum and Rachel has been listening in on his conversation. So, I have no choice but to tell them all my plans. I call everyone down the stairs as soon as Daniel hangs up the phone.

'You okay dude?' I ask.

'Yeah, I am fine.'

I sit all the kids down and tell them of my plans to go away for a while, I don't say that I am moving to Ireland with my Mum, but I do tell them that she is moving over and has invited Lucy, Harry and myself to go and stay with her for a while.

'I think it will do you a world of good,' Elise says.

'Can I come with you?' Rachel jokes, but I am wondering if there is some truth in it.

'Whatever,' Carl says before heading back out of the room.

'He will be fine, but I do think you are doing the best thing,' Elise hugs me.

She is very grown up lately, and I was worried about telling her the most, but she seems fine with the thought of us getting away for a bit.

'I couldn't leave my mum. Otherwise, Rach and I would have come with you.'

They seemed to take the news a lot easier than I expected, and I am starting to feel excited at the prospect of the unknown.

I have been on Facebook and messaged a few of my old friends and told them that I would be back in Ireland soon.

The response I get back is lovely.

Friends who I haven't spoken to since I was a child have said they cannot wait to see me again. For a change in my life, I am feeling wanted. I know more than anything that I need to get away, not just for me, but for my two youngest as well.

Lucy has started playing up, and I don't feel like I have any support with her lately. Rachel and Carl both refuse to look after her while I am down at the shop, and the shop is doing that shit lately, that I can't see walking away from it will affect me as much as I first thought. Harry, on the other hand, has got really withdrawn and quiet. I hate seeing my kids like this and I think being in this house is a constant reminder of what we have all lost. Harry refuses to talk to his older siblings this past week; I am hoping it is a phase and that he will be fine before we leave. As for me, I am the only person he seems to want to have a conversation with, and even at that, it is a mere whisper, and I have to ask him to speak up.

A few months break I know will do us a world of good, and with my Mum accompanying us, I believe we will be okay.

FRESH STARTS AND FRIENDLY FACES...

The day has finally come, and I am saying my goodbyes to the big kids. Daniel has agreed to stay at the house for a few weeks while Rachel and Carl transition their move back down to their Mother's house. Carl is still awkward with me, and I do understand that in his eyes I am taking his brother away from him, but these kids have had months to show me that they want me here and all Carl has done is, lie to me, cause a hell of a lot of arguments with all of us, spat in my face and called me a whore on many occasions, and I am having to remind myself of that when he starts another argument as I am heading out of the door.

'You're just a slag who is running off to get yourself laid,' Carl shouts down the stairs at me.

'I think he forgets who he is talking to,' I say to my brother.

'Oi, I heard that!' Carl bellows as he comes down the stairs to say his piece.

'I know you have been talking to that man all fucking week; you think that I am stupid,' his face is next to mine as Daniel shoves my stepson away.

'No need to get physical,' Daniel snaps.

'I have been talking to a few of my old friends Carl, not that it is any of your business,' I state.

'None of my business? You are leaving and taking my brother away just, so you can get yourself fucked. Stupid fucking whore bag.'

I can see that Carl is upset, but there really is no need for him to be so nasty. The boy reminds me of all the men I have encountered in the past, and I am refusing to let anyone treat or talk to me the way my Father did.

'You are just a slut,' he hisses.

'Enough now Carl, why make this any harder than it already is?' Rachel has heard how her brother is talking to me and stepped in.

'Our Dad has been dead less than a year, and she is already wearing makeup, going out all the time and now fucking other men. She is the only person making anything hard,' Carl is pointing in my face and has taken another step towards me.

'Go get yourself fucked, but don't expect any of us to be here when you come running back!' he snaps before punching the kitchen door.

'I am going before he does something he may regret,' I say hugging Rachel and Elise.

Daniel walks outside with me and explains that Carl was up all night playing on his Xbox and that he hasn't had any sleep.

'He will soon calm down,' he says hugging me goodbye.

I haven't booked my taxi yet, but I decided to ring it from out the back, I just hope Carl stays indoors. Lucy is hugging me; the poor child has seen all the arguments these past few months and has just informed me that Carl scares her.

'He is all talk love, just ignore him,' I say placing my arms around her.

You can tell it has gotten worse this past few months, for my ten-year-old daughter to say she fears her older brother I felt bad and this was not the life I want for either of my children. I ring my taxi, but we have a few minutes wait, the whole time my eyes are on the front door. Waiting to see if Carl will come out to us, but he doesn't.

Mum has already packed all hers and my little sisters bag, she doesn't look like she is taking much, and I know how hard it must be leaving everything behind, but my Mother looks relieved and excited.

The past few hours stress is lifted as soon as my Mother, and I talk about Belfast. My phone has been going none stop as well. It has been nice to learn the world of social media finally. The family member I haven't spoken to in years has reached out and sent me messages online. A few of my old friends have been messaging too. Facebook has been a God send and honestly brought me out of the depression I could feel myself falling into. As much as I know it is not going to be easy, I am looking forward to starting afresh with my children.

'Is that Dylan again?' Mum asks.

'It might be,' I tease.

Dylan is my old best friend and my first ever boyfriend. He was one of the first people to find me on Facebook and we have been talking every day for the past few weeks. I wasn't going to tell him that I am coming over, the plan was to wait until I was there and invite him out to lunch or something. Mum has already offered to have my kids for me while I go out. She says it is her way of giving me back my childhood, whatever that is supposed to mean.

I cannot hold it in anymore, and I had messaged Dylan and told him I would be in Belfast by tomorrow. As you can imagine he has been messaging none stop since. We haven't spoken in over eighteen years, so you can imagine that we have had a lot to catch up on. He was also the first person on Facebook who I had told about what happened with Stuart last year. Being able to write the words down I think made it easier to get it out of me. Dylan has been so nice to me, and I think talking with him has honestly helped me a lot.

'Dylan has said that he cannot wait to see me, after all, this time,' I say. I can feel my face beaming.

'Well I know you said you feel bad for talking to him, but you have nothing to feel bad about Sarah,' Mum says knowing what is going through my head.

'I know Mum, but I do feel bad. Like Carl said this morning; Stu has been dead less than a year.'

'What are you doing wrong?' she asks.

'Nothing, but just the fact that Dylan is making me smile is enough to make me feel guilty,' I explain.

'Oh, stop it now!' My Mother is shaking her head at me.

'Sarah, honestly love, you need to let yourself move on.'

'Less than a year Mum,' I say reminding her.

'Till death do you part; they were the vows to took, and from where I am standing, you held up your end of the bargain.'

She is right, and it is not as if I asked to be widowed at the age of thirty. Had Stuart still been here today then fair enough, but he isn't, and the only person holding me back is myself.

Dylan has been very flirty this week and I have to be honest and say that he has my hormones running wild. I have gone from being expected to have sex in one way or another, almost every single day throughout my whole marriage to nothing at all for eleven months. My entire life in some way or another has been about sex, and it is only now, that I am not expected to do it all the time, that I am starting to miss that connection. Obviously, I do not miss the controlling side to my late husband, but I do miss his touch, his voice and the feel of him beside me in bed.

Mum thinks I am just missing being with someone and that I could do with getting back on the horse, as she puts it.

I am not saying I am thinking about Dylan in that light as such, but I have agreed to meet up with him for a drink one of his evenings after work. He has said that it would be interesting to get to know each other properly as adults. So, I guess that he doesn't have any love interests at the minute. He knows all I have been through lately, and even though he has been flirty with me, he has remained a gentleman too. I am not saying anything will happen between us, but a part of me is excited to find out if it does.

My Mother seems to think that it is some fate bringing us back into each other lives, but I am keeping a very open mind. I have two little people to think about in all of this and Stuart wasn't just my Husband, he was their Dad, and I will not let them know anything about my social life, especially one that may or may not involve a man. Mum and I change the subject as Lucy walks into the kitchen.

'What time are we going tomorrow?' Lucy asks.

'We are leaving here about nine,' Mum tells her.

'Oh, in that case, I think I will get an early night,' Lucy says surprising me.

Lucy has been well behaved these past few days and I am starting to see a grown-up side to my little ten-year-old girl, and I realize how quickly she will keep growing in front of my eyes. I smile at my daughter and pull her in for a hug.

'Goodnight sweetheart,' I say kissing her on her forehead as she leans in and embraces me tightly.

'Ni Night Nanny' Lucy says turning towards the doorway.

'Goodnight Lucy.'

'Love you both,' Lucy shouts from the hallway.

'We love you too,' I shout back. 'Harry time for your bedtime too,' I can hear him talking to his sister on the stairs.

Missed opportunities...

We are all up early and just about to leave Mums when the door goes. It is Craig who has come to say goodbye to me before I leave. He informs me that Sharon is up at my house helping the girls pack away their father clothes.

I never got around to going through his stuff. It just ended up staying where he had left them. Not down to laziness but because when I did try and tidy up, Carl would take it as a personal insult that I was taking his Father's memory away from something. I think now it was just a reason for him to snipe at me and a reason to raise his voice. I don't know if I can put it all down to grief because even when Stuart was alive, Carl was very hot and cold with me.

'I think Sharon said she would keep hold of a few of Stu's things, if you don't mind?' Craig says, but I don't see how I could say no anyway. I was willing to leave it all behind.

'Don't you think it is a little weird all the stuff she is saying?' I ask.

'Yeah, but this is Sharon,' he says placing his hand on his head, 'Sure she now says they were engaged.'

'Who? Stuart and Sharon?' Mum asks sounding shocked.

'Oh yeah, they had it all planned out for years apparently,' Craig sounds as convinced as me about it all.

'She is basically your wife, and she is saying she was having an affair with your best mate. What planet is she on?' I am getting angry that he is so calm about it all.

'I don't know what to believe anymore, but I am leaving her,' he finally says.

'I don't mean to sound like a bitch, but I think you will be getting a lucky escape.'

I know how bitchy that sounded, but in the same breath, that horrible woman has caused me nothing but trouble since I first set eyes on her. Stuart had been telling Craig to leave her for so many years, but Craig seemed fearful of her. At least this way he had a way to get out of the relationship but said he didn't believe what she was saying was true.

'Anyway, you look after yourself kiddo, and between you and me. I think you are doing the best thing. I wish I could get away from this place,' he laughs and makes his way down the garden path just as our taxi pulls up.

'Belfast here we come!' I say excited and nervous at the same time as we all pile into the back of a black cab.

The train to the airport is delayed by over half an hour, and I am not impressed. It is the middle of February, and it is bitterly cold. Our little train station has a small waiting area which would keep us out of this snow had it been open, but it is just my luck that the one day we need it, the staff has locked it up.

'I wish this train would hurry up,' Mum says getting frustrated with the kids who are now starting to play up.

'Come over here please Lucy,' I say to my daughter, but she just gives me a lovely grin and says 'No!'

'Oh, she is a cheeky little Madame lately,' Mum says.

In all honesty, since Stu passed away Lucy has been a handful, I am hoping that moving away will help me get her back on track. Lucy has always tried to test my patience, but she has raised the bar lately, and it is taking all my strength not to spank her bottom. Finally, the train is here, only forty minutes late.

We arrive at the airport with plenty of time to spare, or so I believed. My sister had decided it was her time to start playing up and she had both my Mum and me running around the duty-free shops after her. When we had finally calmed her down, and all three kids were calm we made our way towards the check-in counter. The queue was massive, and I was starting to worry about the time.

'Stop worrying will you?' Mum said, but that was easier said than done.

When we checked in after waiting for what seemed like a forever standing in line, I was told that I needed to take my heavy guitar to the other check-in desk. This worries me slightly as I had fears that my beloved guitar would end up on a different plane. I have owned this guitar, for just under ten years now and it is my oldest precession. I would be distraught if I ever lost it.

Finally, we are ready to head to the gate, but we need to go to the toilet first as Lucy has declared she is about to pee herself. When we return from the bathroom, I cannot see my mum or the kids anywhere, until Lucy points to the café a few feet away. Coffee is just what is needed to calm my nerves.

'Thank you, Mum,' I say as I am passed my cardboard cup.

'We need sugar,' she replies.

Just then I can hear the last call for our plane, so we head to the main waiting area of the airport to see where we have to go. The airport is busy, and my Mum looks like she is struggling to keep up with me. So, I offer to wheel her bag, while she takes Harry's hand instead. I could tell Harry didn't want to take his Nan's hand, but I just explained to my son that we need to be quick otherwise we were going to miss our flight.

After having our bags checked and having to be searched, I am sure we are about to miss the plane, and I am starting to get annoyed. The woman who is patting me down has insisted that we still have time to make it to the gate if we are quick so as soon as our shoes are put back on, all five of us are darting towards the terminals.

'I can see the plane!' Mum shouts from just in front of me.

Her bag is heavy, and my arm is starting to think that she has her whole house in this thing, what with the weight of the damn thing. I push myself a little harder as we approach the large glass door.

'I think we're okay now,' I say panting as we get to the gate.

The stewardess has locked the door. I can still see the other passengers walking onto the plane. I knock on the door to get her attention, but she just shakes her head at me.

'You have got to be kidding me,' I knock the glass door again.

'This is our plane; please let us on,' I beg.

'You are two minutes late, and I cannot let you board the plane, you will have to get on the next plane.'

Her voice sounds muffled, but I am sure she can hear me clearly when I tell her she is a fucking joke.

'Some people are so up themselves!' I snap, not at anyone in particular. I am furious.

'It is okay Sarah, calm down, we can get the next flight,' she said.

'It is not okay Mum. She could have let us on that plane.'

'I know but come on we can get this sorted.'

I know my Mother is right, but I just want to explode. I don't think I have been this angry for a long time and it has just been one thing after another this morning. I am starting to wonder if it is worth all the hassle.

I have agreed to stay where I am with the bags and the kids while Mum goes and tries to salvage our trip. I would honestly feel lost without her. The kids are bored and starting to get annoying; fighting and arguing over stupid shit.

I don't want to snap at them, so I just switch off and grab my phone out of the side of my bag. I have had four messages, wow I am popular today. I smile when I see that one of the messages is from Dylan, but I open the other messages first. Rachel has sent me a goodbye message which has me feeling bad for leaving them behind, but then I am annoyed when I see a message off Carl.

He is very vocal about how vile he thinks I am and that he will fight to have my son taken off me.

I don't respond because if I do I will regret anything that I want to say to him. The other message is from my brother Daniel telling me that I am being slated all over Facebook.

I reply asking who, but already I know it is either Carl or Sharon. They are the only two people I know who have a problem with me.

I was right the first time, Carl has very publicly aired his anger and made it evident to everyone how much he hates me. I need to respond to the post, but just as I start to type, I can see two people have already commented. Rachel has written a big paragraph about how her brother hasn't helped the situation and that him airing it all over Facebook is a very childish thing to do. The next comment is from Sarah; she is the wife of Michael and someone who I thought of as a friend. She has agreed with Carl that I shouldn't be running away and that I have dealt with the whole situation badly but tells him to not be so hard on me. Now I don't know what to write.

I type my text, reluctant to push send, but I do. It reads:

'I am so sorry that you feel this way, and I understand that you are grieving, but I do not deserve this harsh treatment. Your behaviour over these past few months has been out of control, and I will not let anyone treat me the way that you have. I may look like I am running away, but I am doing what is best for my children, and it is not as if I have left you to fend for yourself. Carl, you are eighteen years old and have a Mother who wants you home. So, I will not feel guilty for leaving, and I hope one day you will learn to forgive me xoxo'

I get a reply almost straight away from my cousin Katie telling me to ignore Carl's nasty words, but it is hard to ignore. Carl's response is just to tell me that I bring shame on his family and he has no idea what his Father ever saw in a slag like me. I don't need to respond because I have enough people now commenting on the post.

I finally open my message off Dylan who is complaining about being stuck in work. He works for a tailor making old suits and sounds like a fascinating job if you ask me. Dylan is very work motivated which is a good thing.

It does mean that I know so much about the ins and outs that go into a suit now. I reply to him and explain how interesting my morning has been so far.

'Shit, and I thought I had a bad morning x x,' he replies.

I am in the middle of replying when I notice my Mum walking back towards us, she doesn't look happy, so I am guessing it isn't good news.

We have been informed that we can indeed get the next flight over to Belfast, but it isn't leaving until nine the next morning. I explain to my Mum that I have money in the bank if we want to get somewhere to stay overnight.

'Wait, it gets worse,' she says.

Oh, Great! I feel like my chest has fallen into my stomach as I wait for her to carry on.

'They also said that we would have to pay another four hundred pounds for changing the flights,'

'What?' I am shocked.

'Did you explain that we were here on time, but the woman wouldn't let us on?' I ask.

'Yes, I even told them how the boarding app wouldn't work so we were told to wait to the side while others were checked in before us,' Mum says.

'That is crazy. I wouldn't have the money for that as well,' I am defeated and ready to give up.

'May as well go back to yours,' I say with a heavy heart.

'Oh, love you have spent a fortune getting us here, we can't give up now,' Mum places her hand on my shoulder. I don't know why but I shudder at her touch.

We head to the information desk to get a second opinion, but we are told the same, we can pay for new flights, but we cannot get a refund for the plane we have just missed. Even though I have told them how delayed the whole check-in process was, they have regretfully informed me that there is nothing they can do to help.

'Five hundred pounds down the drain, just like that,' I say as I return to my Mother who is looking very stressed out.

'These kids are driving me crazy,' she snaps. 'Sorry love, I am angry for you.'

'Don't be angry for me. You should be annoyed that we have missed the stupid plane yourself.'

'I am, but I didn't have to spend anything, I have lost you all that money, and now we can't go' she says.

'Mum it is only money, we can just go back to yours and figure out a plan B.'

I already have plan B in my head. I get more money in the bank on Tuesday, and if we just wait until then, we can get the boat over. It is another four days away, but I am sure we will all cope at my Mums for a few days more. I explain my plan to Mum as soon as we are in the taxi and heading to the train station.

'Are you sure?' she asked, 'I have no money until next week.'

'I know Mum, don't worry about it.'

LET'S TRY AGAIN...

Tuesday has come quick enough, and we are finally on the boat and heading over to Belfast. Over the weekend I had to talk myself into sticking with the plan. I was ready to say fuck it to the whole thing and go back to the house that I shared with Stuart. Mum kept me sane when I was faltering. Had I returned to my marital home it would have been in spite of myself, a punishment for even wanting to leave in the first place, I feel angry with myself, and I don't know why. I should be happy that I can get away and try and start afresh for myself and my children, but I feel like shit. Mum says it is just because of how nasty Carl has been towards me, but its real reason is down to the dream that I had last night. Stuart was in it and telling me that running away from him, won't stop him haunting me and that he will never forgive me for splitting his family apart.

I know it was just a stupid dream, but it does make me wonder what my late husband would be saying if he was still here. Well, I wouldn't be on this boat, I can tell you that much.

'Are you okay?' Mum asks breaking me from my trance.

'Yeah, I just feel bad is all.'

'I have told you, Sarah, you have nothing to feel bad about, you deserve to have a life,' she says 'I know losing Stu wasn't what you expected to happen, but it did. Least you are doing something about it, instead of letting the grief kill you off too.'

Tears start to run down my face as my Mother places her hand on my shoulder. 'It will take time, but you will be okay,' she says.

I feel numb to her touch. I can picture a Mother and daughter hugging so tightly. The Mother holding her child as she weeps into her embrace, but that is all in my head. My Mother has her hand on my shoulder patting me as if I am a dog, saying there, there, 'You will be okay'.

Yeah, I will be, but that will be down to me I remember thinking to myself as I wipe the tears away. Just in time too, as Harry appears from behind the climbing frame.

'Love you mummy,' he says.

That is all I needed to give myself a kick up the arse. I walk over to Harry, pick him up and tell him that I love him too. We then spend the next hour running around the play area finding the girls, who are hiding.

It is almost two in the morning and the boat will arrive in Belfast in just over four hours. With all the kids fast asleep I tell my Mum that I am going to try and do the same. It isn't easy when the lights are all on, and you have a small chair to try and get comfortable in, but I eventually fall asleep.

We are woken by the speakers above our heads. We have just docked, and the passengers are getting ready to leave the boat. My Mum and the kids are still fast asleep, so I wake them with urgency and start gathering our belongings.

'Come on sleepy head,' I say to Lucy who keeps trying to bury her head to sleep. 'Otherwise, you are going to end up sailing back to England on your own.'

She soon darts up and starts to get her shoes on, one eye still closed.

'Are we ready?' I ask very sleepy looking children. I get a few grunts and a nod in return.

'Oh Jesus, it is cold,' Mum says as we walk off the back of the boat.

'I wish we had of got a cabin last night,' I say noticing the ache in my back from sleeping upright.

'Oh, I know, but sure we will sleep tonight,' she says.

I didn't know the plan from here, and Mum had said that I don't need to worry and that the local council would have us in our own place within a matter of hours. I guessed she had already sourced a house while we were still in England.

As it turned out, Mums plan was to go to the housing and tell them that we are homeless, she explained when were where standing outside the big imposing brown building that she had told them a little white lie.

'What did you tell them?' I asked.

'I said that we were getting away from violent relationships,'

'You did what?' I am shocked, but this is my Mother all over, and I should have known.

'I said that Gaz was trying to beat me and take your sister off me, and I said you were getting away from Carl,'

'Mum really, why did you have to say that?'

'So, that they would help us, Sarah, just go with it please.'

'Looks like I have no choice,' I say annoyed that she has put me in this situation 'If I had of known all this Mum,' I say, but she just tells me it is for the best.

Four hours of waiting around and having to make up a lie about how my step son was being abusive and threatening me were taking its toll on me. I am so tired and annoyed that we have to wait so long.

Eventually, I am seen, and it transpires that they want to put my Mum in a hostel the other side of Belfast and leave me here up north. I am not going to be staying in this country on my own, in a place I don't know.

'I would rather go back to England,' I say to the man giving me the interview.

'So, you are saying that you want to stay with your Mother and sibling?' he asks.

'If that is an option, then yes.'

I am left in the room with Lucy being irritating due to sheer boredom for over half an hour when the man finally returns.

'We may have sorted it, if you want to wait outside, I will call you back in when I know more,' he says as I get to my feet.

'This takes the piss a little,' I say to my Mum when I join her outside for a cigarette.

'I know, but it will be sorted soon.'

Within an hour we are in a taxi and being taken to a woman's refuge. We are told that no men are allowed at this woman's hostel and that we will be given separate rooms, but at least we are remaining together.

'Honestly Mum, I would have got the next boat back, if I was sent anywhere without you.'

'I know, but least it is sorted now,' she says.

The hostel is a massive building just like all the others on the street. I am unsure if I am nervous but the imposing buildings either side of the road are not filling me with the nicest of thoughts. This looks like a rough street, and as much as I know, it has all calmed down considerably since I last lived in this country. The worries of being an outsider are weighing on my mind. My Mum can see that I am worrying and has told me to arrange to meet up with Dylan after work so that I can get away from all the stress for a few hours. I tell her that I am okay and that I am sure that Dylan will have plans anyway.

Dylan has been messaging me all day, and it is nice to finally have a little bit of good news to tell him. He replies straight away telling me that he cannot believe that he will get to see me in person real soon.

I tell him that my Mum has offered to have my kids when we do meet up, and he has asked me when I am free.

'I told you, that you could go out with him later if you want to,' Mum says when I tell her of my messages.

I don't respond to my message straight away as the taxi driver helps us to the door with our bags. I go to get my purse out to pay him, but the driver informs me that it is paid for by the hostel.

Once inside we are introduced to a small dark-haired woman who is in charge of the hostel. She has told us that our rooms will be ready in a few minutes and has asked if we can fill out some forms while we wait. Just all my personal information and a form to claim housing benefit. It says on the form that we will have to pay fifty pounds each on arrival. I know my Mum hasn't any money until Thursday, so I tell her that I will pay for her room as well.

'Oh love, thank you, you know I will pay you back,' she says.

Dylan has been texting me again and I have agreed to meet him for an hour later today. I am nervous at seeing him in person after so long and almost ready to back out. That is until Lucy starts with her attitude. She has been in a bad mood all day and my patience is wearing thin. It isn't fair on my daughter if I end up losing it with her, so I tell myself that a few hours break from the kids will have been well and truly earned.

'As long as you are sure Mum?' I say needing the added reassurance.

'For God's sake, if you don't go and meet him, I will,' she snaps slightly, but I know that is down to the kids playing up.

Dylan said he knows where my street is, and that he will be waiting at the bottom of the road for me, at half five. I am a little nervous but at the same time it is very laid back between the two of us, and we have been speaking every day now for months.

We were bound, to meet face to face soon enough.

I had told Dylan last month that I was planning a weekend break over here in April and now I am here for the foreseeable. Dylan does seem very excited about seeing me, and it is a nice feeling to have.

I am taken to a large bar in town, Dylan has gone to the bar and ordered our drinks. It was weird because for a minute, and I had forgotten what I drink. Stuart would have had a drink every single night, whereas I only really drank on special occasions. This is a special occasion though; it isn't every day that you go out for a drink with your first crush. Dylan was my first ever boyfriend when I was eleven years old. Just the sweet innocent type of love. Back then my head was all over the place, and I couldn't tell Dylan what was going on at home, we would go weeks without seeing each other, for one reason or another and eventually after a year, we called it a day. That was over eighteen years ago now, and it is weird, but I feel like I can see that little boy still in there, hidden with facial hair and laughter lines. Dylan walks back to the table with our drinks and wearing a massive smile.

'What has you smiling?' I ask.

'You,' he says leaning in to kiss my cheek.

'Well, I wasn't expecting that,' I blush.

'Sarah, I never thought this day would come, and I am blown away. You still look the same as you did when we were kids,' he says sounding shocked.

'So, do you Dylan.'

'No, I look old compared to you,' he smiles.

'Smoke?'

'Yes please.'

The smoking area is not what I had expected. The walls are all painted in stylish graffiti style artwork, and substantial sixty-inch screens hang either side of the outside bar.

'Wow you don't get places like this in England,' I

say looking all around me. The fairy lights add to the sense of calm around me, and the live music is slightly drowned out making Dylan easier to hear.

'So, am I what you expected?' Dylan asks me.

Well what I am supposed to say, that is one of those questions that you ask for the sake of it, of course, I would never have known what to expect, and therefore I cannot have an opinion, but instead, I smile at him and ask the same question back.

'I think you are what I expected, maybe a little shorter,' I tease. 'What did you think when we first started talking, was I what you expected?'

'Not at all Sarah, nearly all our old mates have put on seventy stone and had like ten million kids. I am not saying that is what I expected, but I just didn't expect you to look the same as we did when we were kids is all.'

'Aww, thank you, but you don't have to be nice for the sake of it,' I joke.

'Your bum is a little bigger than I remember,' Dylan smiles as I sit down on the bench beside him.

'Cheeky,'

Dylan then places his hand on my leg, and I think about moving it out of the way, but I don't.

'Sarah, can I kiss you?' he asks.

'You don't waste any time,' I am a little lost for words, we have been in each other's company for less than an hour.

'Don't you think you are being a little forward?' I ask.

'Yes, but I was twelve when I last kissed you, and I would just like to see how it feels now that we are both adults,'

He is cheeky, but it works as I move in for a kiss.

DRINKING BUDDIES...

It has been a little hard to settle in this hostel and I am trying to keep myself to myself. That is hard when you are sharing a twenty-bedroomed property with twenty other women and their children. Being in a woman's aid hostel as well means that everyone in here is living here for a reason. Some have been housed here by social services due to one reason or another but usually to do with drugs. Other women are here because they are in hiding and most have recently got out of an abusive relationship. This is a breeding ground for the anti-male brigade. Everyone has a story to tell apart from me. The real reason I am here is purely down to the fact that I refused to be put in a different hostel to my Mother. My Mum and I are here because we are homeless, but every evening we are probed for information. If it isn't the other residents asking why we are here, it is the staff wanting to be noisy. I have just said I moved away to start afresh somewhere new, but it turns out that Mum has told everyone how controlling my dead Husband was.

Nothing she has said is a lie, but I am still miffed that she has been talking about me behind my back. Less than a month we have been here, and I am being asked by staff if I am willing to talk yet. Talk about what? I don't need to talk to anyone.

Mel is on shift tonight. She is the main member of staff who greeted my Mother and I the first night we moved in. She is nice enough but seems rather firm in her approach. I am annoyed when she informs me that she is taking my kids off for an hour tomorrow to give me a little break. I haven't asked for a break, and when I ask Mel what she is talking about, she informs me that the staff must do it once a month to check on the children's welfare.

I have taken this as a personal insult, and I have told Mel that my kids don't need to be checked. She then snidely tells me that every child under her roof will be checked. That evening I am outside with some of the other Mums, it is almost ten in the evening, and all the kids are fast asleep in their rooms.

We have a small intercom, so we can hear if the younger ones wake up.

I am still fuming with Mel and ask the girls if they have had the same treatment? It turns out Mel is the only member of staff who does these little meetings. She calls it 'helping hands' and says it is a form of therapy for the kids.

'My daughter told me that she was asked if I hit her,' Sue says before lighting her third cigarette in the last ten minutes.

'Yeah, my Tony banged his knee, and I was asked a hundred and one questions about how he got the bruise. Like, he is five, what do they expect?'

'Mum I feel like we are being punished for being here,' I say. 'I am going to start looking for a private rent.'

'You may as well,' Nicole says, 'I have been here three years and still no closer to getting our own place.'

Nicole is from Poland, and she has had a tough time claiming benefits and any other help that most of us are entitled to. Nicole has three girls who were all born over here, but because after Nicole split with the girl's Father due to violence, she went back to Poland for a few months. It turned out that if she had stayed in Belfast, she would have been fine, but she went home for a while, so now she is in the same boat as any other foreigner travelling over and making themselves homeless.

For the next three Sundays, my kids are taken into the art room for an hour and a half and asked lots of questions. Lucy says that they are mainly trying to find out about Stuart and that they have asked a few times if I smack them for being naughty.

I have smacked my children, but not to hurt them, to scold them when they are really pushing it. I would never be too hard on them, as I know what it is like to fear getting hit. I will never let my children ever feel that type of fear from me. Even with that in mind, I am still worried that they are trying to take my kids away.

I shouldn't have been worried about what my kids were going to say.

It was my own drunken talking that nearly cost me everything.

It is a Friday night, and only Sheila is working this evening. Sheila is laid back and doesn't mind us girls, going out and having fun, as long as we don't bring any alcohol back into the hostel. I had planned to go to Dylans house this evening, but he has let me down at the last minute. I could have stayed at home and sulked, but Mum was willing to have my kids in her room with her, so I asked Nicole, Sal, and Sue if they fancy heading into town with me, and they agree. Both Nicole and Sal have their families looking after their children for the weekend, and Sue's daughter is almost sixteen so been told to stay in her room until her Mum returns home. I think this must be a regular thing as Sue's daughter sounds like she has heard her mother say this quite a few times in the past.

'Go and have fun Mum, don't get too drunk,' Sue's daughter said pushing her Mum out of the door.

Don't get too drunk. Well, that really didn't happen. We started off with good intentions, but Nicole had managed to conceal a half bottle of vodka down her bra. She had offered to get us the first round in, which was just little weak mixer drink. In the UK we call them alcopops. It would take at least ten of them to make you even start to feel tipsy. Not when Nicole is in charge. We are each poured half of our drinks into the glass. I haven't tried this funky blue alcohol, so I am told I can take a small swig to make sure I will drink it. It tastes like pure sugar but is drinkable. Nicole then looks all around her to make sure none of the staff can see her. She opens the vodka and fills our drinks up to the top.

'This will sort us out ladies,' she smiles, and we raise our glasses to toast. 'Here's to a well-deserved night out.'

That evening we danced and drank far too much for our body to handle. The last thing I remember was being in the Coocoo bar and asking a ginger guy to dance with me. I was all platonic, but before I knew it, Nicole and Susan are pulling me away.

'I was just dancing,' I tried to say in my slurred-up sentence.

'He was trying to take you home,' Sue says.

'Noooope' I smile. 'Not going to happen.'

'I know, come on, let's go,' Nicole grabs my arm and starts to pull me towards the door.

Once outside the air hits me and I honestly do not remember getting back to the hostel. This only adds to my frustration the next morning when I wake in a puddle of my own sick. I didn't eat anything yesterday.

In all honesty, I haven't been eating properly for months now, but drinking on an empty stomach is not something I plan to do a second time.

Lucy and Harry must have woken up and seen the state of me because I am woken by my Mum asking if I am okay.

'Drunk,' I say keeping my eyes tightly closed.

'The kids came and woke me, and they said the room smells of sick, and I can see why.'

I open my eyes, worried about what sight would be laid in front of me.

'Yuck,' I say looking at the bed and floor with what looks like leftover pizza.

'Oh, I think I am about to throw up again.'

I had been sick so much last night, that it was in my bed, all over the floor and baked into my hair and face. I am mortified that my kids have seen me in this state and I vow never to get so drunk again in my life. I have never been much of a drinker, but last night I was passed free shots for hours so no wonder I am feeling so tender now.

'I will take the kids down the stairs and get them fed, while you have a long shower,' she says ushering my daughter back out of our bedroom.

Harry is already down the stairs.

'Thank you, Mum.'

Once I have heaved my empty stomach that much that I know I have nothing left inside me, I start to clean up my mess. I have never gotten into this state, and I know it won't happen again.

'Feeling fragile?' Sue asks as I make my way to the shared kitchens.

'That is an understatement.'

'I don't even remember getting home from to Coocoo' I say.

'So, you don't remember almost getting arrested?'

'What?' I am shocked.

'Yeah, Nicole was booting everyone's car down the road,' Sue is smiling, so I am unsure if she is pulling my leg.

'Honestly Sarah, we went for pizza to calm her down, but that didn't end well either.'

'I cannot remember even going for pizza,' and I honestly can't.

'So, you don't remember having a food fight?'

'Oh my God, please tell me you are joking?' I want the floor to swallow me whole.

'Nope, no joke, we were crazy last night.'

I walk over to my Mum who is cooking eggy bread for me.

I am mortified, and feeling too embarrassed to even look at anyone, including my kids.

'Sarah, that is the first time I have ever known you to get wasted,' Mum says.

'Oh, and trust me it will be the last.'

I have never believed people in the past when they have tried to say that they cannot remember what was happening when they have been drunk. My ex Greg would use that excuse all the time, and I honestly thought it was a piss arse excuse that was given to try and persuade me to forgive him. I hate that I cannot remember last night and worried that I had acted stupidly in front of these women.

'I won't be going out again in a hurry.'

'Sarah, it makes a change. It isn't as if you could drink while you were married,' Mum smiles but that comment has annoyed me.

'I was allowed, I just didn't drink,' I say defending Stuart.

'Stuart drank enough for the both of us,' I add realising that I have just been over snappy to my Mother.

The real reason I have never been much of a drinker is that I worry that I might say something that I would generally keep inside. I would have less control over my mouth when I drink too much. The last time I had drunk so much, it ended with my Mother and I arguing and a good beating off Gregory as a consolation prize, so I learned my lesson after that. Mum has never believed me; she says that she does but tells everyone else that it is all lies, made up after an innocent encounter in the bathroom.

Now that I have started writing about my childhood, I am beginning to realise how messed up I must be and with my Dad being on my mind these past few weeks, I am scared I may say or do something that I later regret.

Turns out that is wasn't even my mouth I needed to watch. It was a few weeks later while I was having a night out. I had been spending a lot of time with Dylan because he had decided that he was going to emigrate over to Australia for a year and do some travelling. He has said that he wanted to spend as much time with me as possible and had invited me out to his friend's gig in town. I was told that we were heading to an after party and would my mum be willing to have my children overnight.

Mum agreed.

So, I am out minding my own business, while she is in the kitchen with all the other Mums telling them how vile my Father was to us. I was shocked that she even admitted the man used to beat me, but she went a little further and said that my Dad used to rape her and had abused me too. My Mum knows that I am writing my book and I am wondering if that is the reason she has said something now.

My evening with Dylan was amazing, and I really did let my hair down. I was being so well behaved until he kissed me. His lips were soft, and the vodka was taking control, and before I knew it, we were in a taxi and heading back to his. We did end up going to the after party, but that was a few hours later. Dylan was sensual with me, and it took me by surprise. We had both agreed that there was no harm in having protected sex, now that we were both consenting adults, but the reality was something else. It was as if we had both been waiting for this since we were teenagers. Dylan was soft but passionate, and I felt as comfortable with him, as could be. I still made sure my top stayed on and the lights were down low, but that was down to my own insecurities about my body. If Dylan had got his way, he would have kissed me all over. Had I known what I was walking back into at the hostel, I may not have rushed home that morning.

I rang the buzzer on the big intimidating door and waiting for a member of staff to open it. I did feel like I was doing the classic walk of shame in the same clothes that I went out in. I had clean underwear on, but that wasn't the point. And when Judith answered the door and had asked me to go into the living room so that she could have a word with me, I had honestly thought she was going to say something about my Mum having all the kids in her room overnight. We are allowed two nights a week out and have a curfew of nine in the evening while we are staying there, but something told me I was about to get a telling off over something. I was even more confused when my Mum walked into the room with Judith.

'What's happening?' I ask.

'We have received an allegation we need you to either confirm or deny.'

WHAT SHOULD I SAY?

I know what she is talking about by the look on my Mother's face. What am I meant to say? Yes, I can admit it all but how will that impact of my children? Over the years I have met people who have dealt with the aftermath of an allegation. Where the children were being bullied because a family member has been convicted. I cannot put my children through that.

'Sarah, I will be talking to you both in private, can you wait in the office for me?' Judith asks.

Judith scares me a little, not because she seems nasty or anything, I just think it is down to her role in this place. Any person with authority seems to unnerve me lately, and I don't know why.

It is twenty minutes later when I am called into the living room.

'Sarah, please take a seat.'

I can feel my heart in my throat, and I think I am about to be sick, but I tell myself that I need to compose myself. My biggest fear is that if I let myself get too emotional, it may look like I cannot raise my children. This woman's refuge seems to report every mother to social services for one reason or another. I am scared that it is my turn. I am annoyed that Mum didn't ring me this morning and give me the heads up, but I am guessing she wasn't expecting me back so early either.

'Now, I have heard something, but I need to hear it from your mouth do you understand?' she asks.

Of course, I understand, but I just nod at her.

'Sarah, anything you say will be in confidence and will not leave this room. Okay?'

I nod at her again. I can talk for England at the best of times, but I feel muted.

'Can you tell me what your relationship with your Father was like?'

'I am not sure you can call it a relationship,' I blurt out, 'I mean we never really got on.'

'Was he abusive to you Sarah?' I can see her trying to read my body language. I cross my legs just in case they try and shake.

'He used to lose his temper easily.'

I am trying to keep eye contact, but it is like a magnetic pull dragging my eyes to the floor.

'He would take his temper out on my Mum and me from time to time, but that's it,'

'What about other forms of abuse?' she asks, but I shake my head at her.

'Is there anything else you want to add?' Judith starts to jot down what I have just said to her, and I clam up.

'No!' I snap.

'Sarah, anything you say will be in confidence, but if I feel the need to report it, I have to.'

'What to report that my Dad used to smack me, big deal.'

'I know you still have siblings in the home, and with what your Mother has told me as well, we need to check that everything is okay.'

Oh, what have I done? My Dad will know straight away that this allegation has come straight from me, even though he deserves everything he has coming to him.

I still fear him and his threats to have me killed if I ever breathe a word to anyone, when all that shit happened with Greg, and he was shouting about my past to anyone who would listen.

My Dad moved away, taking my brothers with him. Apparently, my Father had been threatened by his drug dealer who had heard the rumours.

I was blamed for a while for my Mum losing out on seeing the boys, but she talks to them all on the phone regularly. Her and my Dad seem to get on better now than they ever did and when she talks about him to me I just pretend that I don't give a shit when I don't. I know my Mum doesn't believe me and I have accepted that, and I am just grateful she is here with me now.

'He will know it is because of me,' I say quieter than I intended.

'No, Sarah. It will be a routine check, and I promise you that your name will not be brought into it in any way,' Judith has her hand on my knee, and I worry she can feel me trembling.

'He is far from stupid and will know I have sent someone to his house,' I reaffirm what I have just said.

'I know this is hard, but wouldn't it make you feel better knowing that you have done something?' she asks.

'But I know my Dad isn't like he used to be,' I say defending him for some reason I cannot fathom out myself.

'It is better to be safe than sorry.'

After a conversation for over half an hour and getting angry that I feel like I have been tricked into talking, I am finally allowed to go and find my Mum and my kids. I am annoyed at my Mum for saying anything, but I need to find out how and why it happened. Mum is outside having a smoke, while the kids are playing on the push along toys in the yard.

'You okay?' I ask as she passes me a cigarette.

'Yes, but what about you?'

'Yeah, I told them he was a bit heavy handed, but that's it,' I say.

'Did you not tell them about the other stuff?' Mum asks.

'No, why would I if my own Mother doesn't believe me?' I am being snappy, but I mean what I say, what is the point in telling anyone if she doesn't even believe me?

'I do believe you, Sarah, I know more happened than I know about, but you don't speak to me about it.'

'What? I have tried to tell you loads of times,' I mutter not wanting the kids to overhear our conversation.

'Well maybe one day we can sit down properly and talk about it,' she says with a smile.

'Yeah you can read my book,' I say sarcastically.

'I will read it,'

I look at her with shock. 'Really?' I ask.

'I think it would be easier to read it, than for you to tell me.'

'Trust me Mum, once you know it all, you will want the man dead!' Any mother would.

'Who says I don't already.'

That's a joke, and she was telling me last night how she needs to lend him fifty pounds next week to pay for some bill he has.

'I have almost finished writing the first book I think.'

'Are you going to publish it?' Mum asks.

'I doubt it, I wouldn't know where to start, but I do think I have written it well considering how bad I did in my GSCE's,' I laugh.

'That was your Dads fault for moving us around so much,' she says.

'Well, thirteen school changes would do it.'

Mum and I were having a bitch about my Dad, and it is nice to feel like she is on my side for a change.

'You do know they are sending someone around to his?' I say worried about the outcome.

'I know but don't worry. He has them round for Mathew all the time with school, and he will just think it is for that again.'

'I hope so,' I reply.

'And even if he does know, he has no way of proving it, and he doesn't know where you are.'

She has a point, and what would he do? He will never admit to what he has done to me, and I could have said a lot more. I think I am annoyed that I haven't, but like I said before, I need to think about everyone in this situation, especially my children.

DREAMS CAN COME TRUE...

I am not sure if I mentioned it before, but I have a habit of dreaming things, and then something similar will happen in real life. It happened a few weeks before Stuart passed away. I had a dream that his spirit had left his body, I remember being so out of sorts when I had woken that I needed to tell him straight away. It didn't matter that it was two o'clock in the morning. Stuart told me I was daft at the time, but then a few days later I had a similar dream where I had let go of his hand while we were both hanging off a cliff. It was just a dream, but it made me feel uneasy at the time, and within weeks Stuart had passed away.

Last night I had dreamt that Dylan had fallen out with me. It upset me because we have gotten close over this past few months and even more so this week. We just seem to hit it off, and I think knowing each other when we were kids has taken the awkwardness away from our friendship. In my dream, he had told me that he wanted us to part ways as he was interested in seeing other women before he heads off travelling. The dream felt so real and like a dick, I messaged Dylan and told him about it. We are meeting up in half an hour, and I wish I hadn't said anything.

We are at Annie's tavern while my Mum has the kids. I have told Dylan that I cannot stay out this evening because my Mum isn't allowed have the kids in her room, but the real reason is that I am still feeling out of sorts and cannot be bothered with a late night.

'I like that you are dreaming about me,' Dylan winks at me and leans down for a kiss.

'It wasn't a nice dream,' I remind him.

'Oh, I know. If I were thinking of dating other girls, you would be the first to know,' he jokes.

'Anyway, you have nothing to worry about. If I only have you for a few hours, then we best make the most of it.'

'Here, here,' I say in agreement.

Dylan walks me to the end of my street and as we are saying our goodbyes and I have remembered the big news I had teased him about this morning.

'I almost forgot to tell you my big news,' I say in between his kisses.

'Oh yeah?' Dylan takes a step back and smiles at me.

'Well, I am viewing a few houses tomorrow, so I should have my own place very soon,' I am beaming.

'I cannot wait to come and visit you in your own house, will be good,' he kisses me again.

'I really need to go, I will see you at the weekend?' I ask.

'Yes, hopefully in your new gaff.'

A PLACE TO CALL MY OWN...

I have been up since four this morning and just couldn't fall back to sleep, not from the lack of trying. Finally, at six I got up. Mum and the kids all got up around eight, and I had breakfast all prepared, and all the cleaning is done. I had even mopped the floor which was on the rota as Mums cleaning job this week. All the residents take turns in cleaning the communal areas.

'I have already mopped the floors,' I say passing her a cup of coffee.

'Oh, thank you, love. You were up early,' she says.

'Very observant Mother, I just couldn't sleep.'

'What time is your viewing?' she asks.

'Eleven, I arranged for the same time the kids are out on this trip, so I didn't have to take them with me,'

The hostel organizes a trip once a month for the kids, to give the Mums a break, and I think it is just, so they can do the helping hands without us knowing. Lucy let slip that the staff asks a lot of questions while they are out. Not that I think we have anything to worry about, I just think it is a little sly.

'I will come with you, if you like?' Mum says.

'I was hoping you would say that, because I have no idea where I am going.'

The kids are collected at ten, and I am ready to head out the door, but Mum is still in her bathroom.

'Mum hurry up please!' I shout into her room.

I would have viewed this place on my own had I known she would take so long to get ready.

I am nervous and really want this flat, but the landlord was very cagey on the phone and said he has people viewing all afternoon. I am not feeling very hopeful.

Finally, she is ready, and we head out the door.

Luckily the place I am viewing is only a ten minutes bus ride away, but I had planned to get there early, now it looks like I will just get there on time.

'I cannot wait to get out of that hostel,' I say once we are off the bus and walking up the street towards the flat I am about to view.

'I know what you mean. I wonder if the landlord has other properties too.'

As we approach the address I have been given, I am wondering if we have the right street. The outside of the house looks massive. It's an old Victorian townhouse with an oversized front door and a big bay window.

'I am guessing it is only the bottom half,' I say to Mum looking up at the three-story building.

Mum is too busy looking down at her phone and doesn't acknowledge what I have said.

A few minutes later and a blue BMW pulls up outside the property. A small grey-haired man appears from the driver's seat. He looks down at the folder in his hands and then stares at me.

'Which one of you is Sarah?' he asks quite abruptly.

I lift my hand as he walks over to shake it.

'Andrew,' he announces before walking towards the door of the property.

'Pleased to meet you,' I reply, but the frosty reception has me wondering otherwise.

We follow Andrew inside, and I am taken back a bit by the vast space of the hallway, tall high vaulted ceilings, has me feeling very tiny in here indeed.

'Wow!' Mum gasps as we walk into the living room, again the space is impressive, and the tall open fireplace is striking with its dark wooden surround and marble hearth. I make my way over to it admiring the wood with my finger-tips.

'It is the same height as me,' I say pleasantly surprised.

Andrew then leads us into the main bedroom, this room is just as big, and I can almost see myself here.

I smile at my Mother, and she smiles back at me.

'I really like it,' she says.

Andrew then shows us the bathroom. This room looks like it could do with a little tender loving care, but with a large corner bath and two main windows I can already picture it the way I would like it.

I am a little disappointed when we are led down three steps towards the kitchen. It seems tiny in comparison to the rest of the building and the cupboards have easily seen better days, but again I can see the potential. After talking with Andrew, he asks me if I am interested, and I am.

Back at the hostel and I can't stop talking about the flat we just viewed, and Mum agrees with me, that it is ideal but with others looking at the property all afternoon, I am half expecting not to receive a phone call back.

'He has a lot of others viewing the flat today, so I highly doubt I will get it,' I say voicing my concerns to my Mum.

'Don't be silly,' she states, 'all landlords say that just to get you to panic into agreeing.'

'Yeah I guess you are right,' I say feeling a little deflated.

I needn't have worried though because just after an hour of being back at my Mums I have a phone call back offering the tenancy and it is arranged that I meet Andrew back at the flat the next day to pay the fees and sign for the flat. Andrew also asks me if my Mum is looking for somewhere as he has a flat a few doors down and has said she is welcome to it, as long as she has a deposit.

I should be happy that I have my own place now, but until I have the keys in my hand, I won't let myself get too excited. Mum has noticed I am looking pretty-low too.

'What is up with your face?' she asks.

'I don't know,' I reply, and I honestly don't.

'I thought you would have been over the moon that you have that flat.'

'I haven't got it yet,' I respond, brushing my hair in the mirror while looking at her in the reflection.

'Well you will have tomorrow, and with any luck, I can get the other place,' she sounds excited, but I know she hasn't got the twelve hundred pounds to pay for a deposit.

'Will you apply for a loan?' I ask.

'Yes, they should give me a few hundred at least, and I can see if the landlord is willing to wait for the rest,'

'Fingers crossed,' I reply.

Andrew doesn't come across as a landlord who is willing to wait for his payment, but I know that I have a few pounds put aside for a rainy day. I could loan my Mum the money myself. I don't tell her that, I will wait and see if she can get it herself first.

That evening after taking the kids out for dinner and making sure all our clothes are packing into the suitcases, I head to bed. It has been a long day, and I have so much to do over the next few weeks that an early night is in order.

The next morning, I watch my little sister while Mum goes and views the property a few doors down from mine. Is it bad that I worry that she will say something stupid to the landlord and mess up our chances? I don't know, I think I am just worried that something will go wrong.

I have gone through the best part of the day in my own little daze, and before I know it, it is five o'clock, and I am meeting back up with Andrew to sign my tenancy.

The meeting was a lot quicker than I expected, and the man seemed to be in a rush so once the cash is handed over and I signed the paperwork, Andrew has passed me my keys and gone again. Leaving me alone in this large flat to ponder over the prospect of finally having my own space again.

Now don't get me wrong it has been nice having the company of my Mum and sister, but I have been in Belfast for months now and looking forward to the peace that comes with living in your own house. No watchful eyes from the staff at womans aid and not having to live with twenty other women. It will be bliss.

I message Mum to tell her I have my keys and even she says that it was a lot quicker than she had expected.

Now I just need to get furniture to fill this vast space, but I know my Mum has been online sourcing second-hand stuff for me, so I am not at all worried. My only exception being a brand-new bed.

The thought of being in a bed and sharing one that a stranger has slept in or even had sexual intercourse in, just turns my stomach a little. Although it is almost six now and the shop I intended on visiting is about to close. Sure, it will still be there in the morning, but I know what I am like. Once I have a plan in my mind, I expect it all to come together quicker than usually possible.

I wouldn't say I am impatient but just very eager to get things done in record time.

I text my Mum to tell her I am on my way back and she informs me that the kids have eaten.

I also text Dylan to tell him I have my own flat now.

Dylan didn't reply so the next morning I message him again, I know he is at work, but that doesn't normally stop him from replying to me.

'Oh well, I have too much to be getting on with,' I say to my Mum who knows I have been messaging Dylan since last night.

'Are you not meant to be seeing him tomorrow?' she asks.

'Meant to be, but I don't know now.'

'Well, I can babysit for you at your own house if you have a bed by then.'

'Yes, you can,' I say all excitedly.

'I put my form in for a crisis loan, I should get a phone call by this afternoon. Fingers crossed,'

'And toes,' I say.

Mum got her loan and the few hundred she was missing I had given her out of my savings pot. Mum and I both spent that weekend moving into our own places. I was fortunate that Mums flat had two sofas in it and she let me have the teal one that was in her living room.

I managed to get a mattress and the flat I viewed already had beds in for the kids and a double bed frame for me, so all that was needed was some mattress protectors and bedding. Both my Mum's place and mine have its own cooker, washing machine, and fridge, so that saved us a lot of money and as you can imagine, I didn't see Dylan that weekend. In fact, it was a week later when I had finally seen him, and that was only because I met with him after work and offered to buy him a drink or two.

Dylan was a little off with me, and by the end of the evening, I was left feeling very used. Within weeks we had gone our separate ways, and I hear he is happily engaged to be married nowadays.

FATHER'S DAY...

It has been almost six months since I have moved into this house and as much as I am loving all this space and no one telling me what I should be doing, I am feeling a little lonely. It is fine when the kids are here, but most of the time they are at school or in bed, and I am finding that I am spending most of the time on my own. It has made me write a lot more, and I can finally say that I have finished my first book. I haven't decided what I want to do with it yet, but I am now reading through it to make sure I haven't made any major mistakes. Reading the words in front of me is like I am reading someone else's story. It is mad, I know that I have been through it all, but it is like I have no emotion attached to it. I am reading this story about this poor girl who has been through so much in such a small space of time, and I have admiration for her, but it isn't like it is me. Every single word in my book is the whole truth from my own memory, yet by changing my name, I can detach myself from it. Maybe that is why I have found it easier than I expected to write it all down? It is my form of therapy.

I told my Mum that my book is finished, and it turned into a big conversation about my past, and she said if she had known about the sexual abuse she would have stabbed him. If she is saying that now, then I would hate to think what she will be like afterwards.

Mum is back with her old boyfriend who she left behind when she moved back to England to support me. It turns out that the two of them had spilt up and it was a coincidence that it had happened just after my husband had died. She and Sam are due round any minute.

'So, when are you going to publish this book?' Sam asked.

I didn't even know my Mum had told him about it, but I like the fact that she has, makes me believe that she is in my corner.

'I don't know, I have looked online, but everyone is asking for a few grand up-front,' I explain.

'No,' he says looking at my Mum and back at me 'If anyone is asking for you to pay then it is probably a con. Publishers pay you Sarah, not the other way around.'

'He is right,' Mum says, 'I had a look online earlier.'

'Well I have only just finished it, so I have no intention of doing anything yet.'

'Anyway love, it was just a quick call, we have loads to do before the kids get home,' Mum says winking at her boyfriend.

'I am sure I do not want to know what chores you have Mum,' I say knowing full well that they are going to have an exercise lesson in the bedroom while they have a quiet house.

It is lovely to see my Mum looking happy again. I think it makes her look younger.

It's only eleven in the morning and I have another four hours before I collect the kids from school. I have no books to read and no expendable income to speak of to go out or do anything. I am just stuck in the house with my guitar to keep me company. It could be worse I suppose. I think I am just feeling a little depressed as it is my birthday coming up, oh and Father's Day.

It will be Harry's first year without his dad around, and he is almost eight now so getting older and asking more questions. He knows it is Father's Day next week because they have been talking about it in school. I think that is why he has been playing up all week for me and refusing to do any work in class. I thought he was going to get us evicted at the weekend when Harry had decided it would be funny to throw sand all over Andrew's car. Of all the people to piss off, our landlord isn't one of them.

I have planned to get some balloons and let the kids write on a gift tag with the idea that they are sending a Father's Day message to heaven. With that in mind, I also place a family photo on my Facebook wall and tagged a few people in it.

It is one of my favourite photographs where Stuart is standing on the bonnet of our old Pajero SUV with Elise, Carl and Jack who is Carl's best friend and Lucy and Harry. Everyone has a big beaming smile on their faces, and Stuart is stood at the back with his arms out like a man very proud of his family. It is a pity I am not in the photograph as well, but someone needed to take the shot.

I smile as I am rewarded with some lovely messages from the people I know back home. My brother, Daniel adds a comment about it being his favourite photo too, and I reply telling him that was why I put it up, we then private message for an hour and he tells me that he is over to visit our Mother soon and that he cannot wait to see me. Some days I do miss being back home, and I think that is just because I am not used to it being just the kids and me.

I don't even think about the photo I have put on social media until a few days later. I am online anyway as I have been receiving notifications all morning wishing me a happy birthday. When I scrolled down, I see that quite a few people including Stuart's children have been commenting on my Father's Day photo.

A woman who I don't know has asked if this is Stuart Irvine in the photograph. I am intrigued to know who she is, so I comment back telling her that it is. She responds a few moments later saying that she hasn't seen him in a while and has been worried. I wonder if she is a customer from work, so I decided to private message her and explained that Stuart passed away just under a year ago. She replies telling me that she had no idea and thought it was weird when he stopped contacting her for no apparent reason. Now I am very curious to know who this woman is.

Can I ask how you know my husband? I type.

'Your husband? You sure we have the same man?'

'Yes, love I am pretty sure who is in my photo-graph!' I say out loud.

'What mummy?' Lucy says looking up from her book.

'Nothing sweetheart. Mummy is just talking to herself again' I say smiling, but really I am boiling under the surface.

Stuart Irvin?

I am floored when I see her response.

Yes, well I think so.

The Stuey I know was NEVER married, he didn't agree with marriage which suited me too. Last time we spoke, he was planning on moving down here and setting up home with me. I cannot believe he has a secret life!!!

I think I am about to explode, but then I wonder whether this is someone playing a sick game. So, I ask her to prove to me that she knows Stuart. I am rewarded with a photo of them both in a very friendly embrace.

I am sorry, I didn't know he was with any-one!! The caption under the photo reads.

The woman is called Paula, and after messaging back and forth for the best part of the day it has transpired that my loving husband is nothing but a lying, cheating piece of shit.

My seven-year marriage must have been a com-plete joke to him. Stuart was having an affair be-hind not just mine, but his whole families back for over five years.

Paula hadn't heard a peek from Stuart since the February before he died. That was the point he quit his job and came to work at the market with me every day.

Paula says she had no idea that Stuart even had any children and he really did keep her in the dark about most things. I think the one thing that annoyed me the most is he used the same chat up lines on her, as he did with me.

Stuart had told her that she reminded him of his first girlfriend Rebecca Ingram and that he was drawn to her because of this.

I looked like Becca, although he used to say I was a lot smaller than he imagined she would have been as an adult. Stuart would tell me that it was fate and we were designed to be together. Now I am left wondering if he has used that line with every woman he has ever been with.

I receive another message from Paula asking where he is buried. At that point, I go into my setting and block her. I am crying again and have been most of the day. Happy birthday to me eh?

BETTER OFF BACK HOME...

Not only has Harry been a little shit lately but now both my children have somehow made enemies with most of the kids on the street. They were playing over in the local parks when I get a knock on my door from one of the parents. Her name is also Sarah, and she is shouting in my face that I need to keep my child on a lead. I don't have much time to ask what she is so angry about when she hisses in my face and calls me an English rat. I am then told to watch my back, and Sarah informs me that no one in the street likes me and that I should fuck off home. I am annoyed but more shaken up than anything. Sarah is a big woman compared to me, and even if she cannot fight, she will knock me out with one punch. Her fist is almost the same size of my head.

As soon as the kids return from the shop, I am like an enraged banshee, wanting to know what the hell has happened to cause so much hassle with our neighbours.

'It was Lucy,'

'No! It was Harry. He was...'

'Mum I didn't do anything,'

'Yes, you did Harry!'

I can't hear anything but kids screaming at each other.

'ENOUGH!!' I bellow, my voice filling our whole flat.'

I cannot deal with this right now and tell the kids to get out the door. I head to my Mums flat with the kids in tow.

Once inside I explain to my Mum that her so-called friend Sarah has been threatening me. Mum says she will have a word with Sarah, but I know what my Mum is like, she will say that she will have a word, but she won't say anything and tell me that she has tried. The last thing my Mum needs is to start a war with the neighbours as well, and I know she thinks it is my fault. I can tell by the way that she is looking at me.

'With Stuart's kids still on at me to go back home, and all this with Sarah. I can tell you, Mother, I am very tempted.'

'Please don't say that,' she says passing me a coffee.

'Cheers,'

'After what you have just found out about Stu, I am surprised you are even talking to his family,' Mum says.

'I cannot take it out on the kids and I have had to tell them that I don't believe Paula. It isn't their fault Stuart is a lying bastard.'

'You are too nice Sarah. I don't believe no one knew about it, not for five years,'

I am in floods of tears now, and Mum just looks down at her phone. Any normal Mother would be cuddling their daughter, but my Mum and I have never had a close relationship, so I don't expect the loving arm now.

She does pass me some tissue paper to wipe my eyes.

Mum has a valid point as well, and I am wondering if Carl did know at least. I don't think the girls would have ever known as I think it would have crushed them as much as it has done for me. Stuart would never have wanted to hurt those girls. I used to be able to say that about myself too.

Carl, on the other hand, has never had any respect for me, and if he knew about his Dad's affair, then it would make a little sense why he would feel this hatred towards me.

'You need a good night out,' Mum says.

'That isn't going to happen,' I moan.

'Even if you have my kids, I have no one to go out with,' I explain.

'You should join this site I am on,' she says showing me her phone.

'I don't think so!' That has stopped me crying and I am now laughing at my Mother.

'Why don't we make you a profile?' Her eyes widened and darted straight at me. I do not like the sound of this.

'No Mum, I'm not sure internet dating is for me.'

She looks gutted and then goes on to explain how much she enjoys the attention, and a nice message from a handsome man was enough to brighten her day and that it doesn't mean I have to go on any dates with these guys.

'Thought that was the whole point, to get me out on dates?' I joke.

After over an hour of talking about this site, she has finally convinced me. Perhaps a little attention would be nice; it's not like I have anyone to tell me I am not allowed. And still seething over Stuart, I think a good night out might be fun.

'Pass me your phone I will sort it for you, if you make us a coffee?' Mum smiles.

Taking over my phone, the woman looks like she is in her element, I honestly haven't seen her look so elated, and it has me worrying slightly.

'I need to add some photos of you,' she explains wanting to look through my gallery on my phone.

'I don't have many recent ones,' and I really don't.

'This one is nice Sarah. The sun makes your hair look red,' Mum says holding the phone in my direction.

'Yes, but I don't look like that anymore,' I say concerned.

The photograph in question is one of me standing on a beach in a black flowing top. It is so sunny that the ocean is glistening behind me. My hair looks a warm ginger colour from the glow of the sunlight and has half covered my face as it had been windy that day.

'I do look good in this photo, it's the best one of me so far, but it is over five years old now and really doesn't look like me anymore.'

'Yes, it does, your hair is just darker now,' she says defending herself as she adds it to my profile anyway.

'Think it should be your main profile picture?' she says waiting for me to agree.

What the hell have I let myself in for? I think to myself.

I would never have dreamt of internet dating before today, and now Mum has me slightly excited about creating this account.

A few minutes pass while my Mum is typing away on my screen.

'It's all done now,' she sounds very proud of herself as she passes me back my phone.

'You might want to read the write up about yourself,' she looks at me and waves her cup and reminding me that I was making a drink for us both.

I peer my head around the doorframe because everyone seems a little too quiet for my liking. The kids are all sat in the living room watching a Disney DVD, and I am glad that they are calm for a change. When I return to the kitchen, Mum hands me my phone back.

I cautiously read what she has written on my profile.

To be fair to her my Mum has written a good paragraph about me, it's not too self-absorbed, but it does make me sound very interesting.

I suppose I am a little interesting after all.

I play the guitar, though I do not claim to do it well. I am creative and enjoy drawing and painting, but again I am very modest and wouldn't have necessarily wrote this about myself. So, I am glad that Mum has taken over, because I don't think I would have known what to write. Even though I am writing a book about my life.

Within a few minutes, I am receiving messages from local men. Most of them are just saying Hi and welcoming me to the site. I am smiling for the first time in a while as I receive message after message.

'Popular?' Mum giggles.

'A little too popular I think. I am guessing there is a shortage of girls on this site?' I joke.

'Not at all Sarah, you are pretty so men will want to know more about you.'

I think that is the nicest compliment my Mum has given me in a long time.

'By the way, your brother should be here for just after seven tomorrow,' she says.

I know he is traveling throughout the day, so I am assuming she means in the evening.

'No worries I will probably see him on Friday because I won't want to bring Harry out after seven, he likes his routines,'

'I know he does.'

The next morning, I am woken by the kids outside. I have slept through my alarm, so I jump out of bed, waking the kids up and then we spend the next half an hour rushing about to get ready for school. Lucy is on a go slow at the best of times, but she is as awkward as ever this morning, and I am trying my hardest not to snap at her. I only put my phone on silent because I was receiving messages most of the evening off men from that dating site, and as much as it is lovely to be getting some attention, it is making me feel a little uneasy. It seemed like the later in the evening it was getting, the cruder the messages were. Why men think we want a photo of their manhood is beyond me, but I did use the block bottom a few times and can see me using it a lot.

Mum rang me to tell me that Daniel was on his way.

She has also admitted to me that she hasn't enough food in to feed her son while he is over. It turns out that she doesn't want to ask my brother for any money to stay with her, so she has asked if she can borrow some money off me instead. Of course, I agree because I will never see her without, but I do explain to her that it is the last of my savings and I will need to start collecting back some of what she owes me. I felt bad even telling her that I will need it back but now we are looking at almost four figures, which may not seem a lot, but when you are not working and bring up children, a grand is a lot.

Mum is due around any minute, and I think it is her knocking on my door, but it is the kids from the street playing pranks again. Harry is playing in the garden, so I check on him before closing my door again. A few moments later my door goes again, and as I open it, Harry tells me that it is one of Sarah's children knocking and that he heard their Mummy telling them to keep beating the door.

'Mum, I think they want you to shout so that their Mum will fight you,' Harry says looking a little fearful.

'Don't worry son, and no one is going to be fighting. I think you should just come in and then you can't be accused of anything.'

Harry reluctantly comes inside to play, but with the sun beaming down on Belfast I don't blame him for wanting to play outside.

'We can go to the park when Nanny has been,' I say trying to soften the blow.

'No point,' Harry shrugs.

'Come on son; it will be fun.'

'I hate living here, why did we even move?' he snaps.

'I want to go back home,' he says.

'This is our home now,' I try to explain.

'Well I hate it, and I don't like this house, and I don't like you for making us live here,' he sobs.

'It won't be forever son,' I say placing my arms around him.

I know a lot of that outburst is just down to him being annoyed that he cannot play outside and the fact that he keeps arguing with Sarah's daughter Erin, but I am still wondering if moving here was the best idea after all.

DATING DISASTERS...

Since my brother Daniel arrived a few weeks ago, my Mum has been pushing me to go out more often. Problem is I have no friends to speak of here. The Mothers from the hostel all have their curfew and no babysitters on hand. Mum had Lucy and Harry for me last weekend and Daniel, and I went out for a drink and a game of pool. It was lovely to get dressed up and go out, but I was with my little brother so anytime anyone even looked at me, Daniel was glaring at them. He knows it has been a year now since Stuart passed, but he still holds loyalty to my late husband and the thought of his sister being with another man just doesn't sit right with him. Which I get. Doesn't stop me wanting to at least go on a few dates, I am intrigued. Any relationship in the past has developed into a relationship at an alarming rate. I moved in with Simon when I was seventeen, and it just turned into a relationship. Greg moved in with me within weeks of meeting me and Stuart and I were married within a year. I want to know what it is like to date a guy. Someone who doesn't need saving in some aspect or another, someone who has their shit together maybe. I don't want a relationship, but I would love to find that someone special who I think I can connect with. I can't do that while I am out with my brother.

I have been on this dating app for a month now, and apart from a few people, most of them seem very immature. I am wondering if I am getting too old for this type of thing. Mum has told me to persevere and has talked me out of deleting the app twice now. A man called Marty keeps messaging me, but I am unsure as he seems a little pushy through his messages. Then there is Kyle who messages me as well, but I knew Kyle when I was younger, and in all honesty, I don't think he is into women. I was very surprised when I started receiving rather naughty messages off a female too, but I kindly told her that I was flattered but not interested.

'Why don't you ask one of these boys out on a date?' Mum says while folding her washing.

'I am not sure I like any of them,' I joke.

'What about that Marty you were telling me about?' she asks

I explain to my Mum that he is pushy, and I don't think I like him but just haven't told him yet. Mum says I need to give him a chance. It turns out she has a big sofa to get up six flights of stairs and that she and Daniel need the manpower. Marty has been bragging about how strong he is, being an ex-army man and now a gym buff. That I don't find attractive at all, but Mum seems to think he is perfect and wants me to ask him over for a drink so that she can get this sofa up the stairs.

That evening Marty comes around, and in all honesty, I felt so uncomfortable just being around him. The sofa took a lot more effort than anyone had intended, and the situation was stressful. Marty seemed to have a short fuse and told me that I owed him a drink after all the aggravation. So, I invited over to mine for a can of beer. Marty had already been to the shop on the way and pulled out a bottle of whiskey from his bag.

'I bought my own,' he says.

Daniel has already given me a knowing look to say that he has my back and Mum has offered to have Lucy and Harry for me, so the three of us walk back over to my flat. Marty is telling us about his time in the Army and how he has a four-year-old daughter who he has never seen because her Mum moved away while he was stationed in Iraq. He tells me that I am lucky to have my children.

'I know I am,' I smile as I open the front door to my flat.

Marty has been here for less than twenty minutes, and already I am worrying because he has downed three small glasses of whiskey. After Greg, and the way he would turn on me after a drink in him, I hate being around drunken people. I especially hate the fact that he is a hundred and fifty pounds of a man and is in my home. No one in my family is big, and Daniel and I would be no match for Marty if he were to turn nasty after drink.

It was an hour later when Marty finally left, but not before trying it on with me and to the point that even my brother had to ask him to leave me alone. Marty finally stormed out accusing me of leading him on. Marty and I had been talking for weeks, and he knew that I was a recent widow and that I wasn't ready to move on. He agreed that he would move the sofa because he wanted to meet my mother after knowing I was off limits, but I was apparently leading him on? I made sure he knew this evening that I wasn't interested in him in that way and that I wasn't ready for a relationship.

Daniel had spent the best part of the evening talking about Stuart which should have been a big enough hint, but Marty was mad that he felt used. He started shouting and slammed his glass on my table before walking out and slamming my front door. The man intimidated me from the second I met him, and I was so grateful that my brother was here.

My second date didn't go much better either. After making my excuses for over two weeks about how and why I couldn't get a babysitter, I finally gave in to him and agreed to go to dinner that weekend. The man in question was called Darren, but when I met him, I almost didn't recognize him. He looked a lot older in real life, and I guessed the photos on his profile were taken a good few years ago. Darren was a delivery driver and was still in his work uniform. As he stood up to greet me with a hug I noticed he had a weird smell about him, and I knew within the first five minutes that it wasn't going anywhere so after we had both finished eating. I had politely excused myself and made my escape, paying my half of the tab on the way out. Darren was still sat at the table waiting on me, but something about him made me feel uneasy so I didn't feel guilty, and he must have got the message because I didn't hear from him again.

I was honestly starting to wonder if everyone on this dating site was the same. Most men just want sex, and I don't know how I feel about that. The last thing I want is a relationship. The last thing my children need is their mother rushing into yet another relationship, but I do miss the company, and I would be lying if I said I am not missing the connection of being with someone. I would generally shy away from a hug or any form of affection, but I think I am starting to crave it a little.

I am in my thirties, widowed with two children and I don't have a job, so I am not the best prospect for anyone really, but in the same breath, I know how lucky a man would be to spend time with me. I think I am finally starting to see my worth. Writing a book about myself has clearly helped me see who I have become and in spite of it all. I am still soft, gentle and kind. The only people who have seen me shout or lose my cool is the kids, but they really do push it some days, and I think every mother can agree with me when I say that our children have more control over our emotions at times than we do. I am such a laid-back person, and I don't feel like I have been able to be my complete self in any relationship myself. I want to meet someone kind who I can still to share experiences with, but I think I need to take this time to figure out who I am. I am so used to being Stuart's wife or before that somebody's girlfriend that I need to find the real me, the real Sarah.

I have blocked so many people on this app, and gently told a few that I am not interested. Others have just stopped messaging because I have forgotten to respond but that suits me. I would delete the app, but I have been messaging a man for the past few hours who comes across as a nice guy for a change. Something about him has made me want to find out more. He is a little cheeky and has had me smiling since his first message. His name is Adam, and he has recently returned home from studying overseas. Adam is a little younger than me but insists that he likes an older woman. I have warned him that I don't look my age and still need to make sure I have my ID when I go out because of my height and build.

Adam took the time to read up on my profile, and he has asked if he can hear me play the guitar one day soon.

I agree, but we have been speaking for a few hours, so neither of us knows how that will develop or if we will even like each other.

Adam has just made the mistake of asking what has brought me over to Ireland and I think about just telling him that it is because my Mum lives here but if he does get to know me better, he will know I have lied. I am honest and tell him that I became a widow just over a year ago and wanted a fresh start for my kids and I. Part of me is expecting him to run a mile now and I couldn't blame him either. My phone goes quiet for the first time in three hours.

It is an hour later when I get a response telling me that he was sorry for the late reply, he had to go to the shop for his mother and had left his phone at home. Adam didn't need to tell me that, I already knew that information would take a while to sink in and I am just happy that I have had a message back.

It's okay, and I was cooking dinner anyway I type.

Adam then asks what I was cooking, and when I tell him, he says he is offended that I didn't offer him some food.

You have a Mummy to cooks yours... I type.

Doesn't mean she will, I cook my own food now that I am a big boy lol

Adam and I are messaging most of the evening, and he has sent me a goodnight message just as I head to bed. It makes me smile because I have never really received a goodnight text.

It is a few days later when Adam asks me out for a drink. Initially, I think he means the weekend or something, but it transpires he means that evening. Daniel is around visiting, and the kids are fast asleep. It is only just gone seven at night, but it has been a hot, sunny afternoon and I think the heat has taken it out of them. My brother and I have just sat down to watch Avatar for the tenth time this year. I don't respond to the message straight away.

'So, that lad I have been messaging has asked if he can take me out for a drink,' I say to my brother feeling slightly embarrassed.

'Oh, that good sis,' he smiles 'look, I know I said what I said about you moving on and all that, but at the end of the day I just want you to be happy.'

'I know you do.'

'When are you going to meet this man then?' he says sitting himself up on the sofa.

'Well he did ask if I was busy tonight, but I haven't messaged him back yet.'

'Well then what are you waiting for?' my brother points to the hallway, 'Go get yourself dolled up,' he smiles.

'I don't think I am ready to meet him yet,' I am feeling nervous just at the thought, 'He seems too good to be true.'

'Look sis, the kids are sparked out, and I honestly don't mind sitting here all night. What have you got to lose?' he asks.

'My entire faith in men if tonight turns out as bad as my dates have so far,' I mutter. 'I'm just not sure Daniel. This one seems nice, and I don't want to mess it up by meeting him too soon. We have only been speaking a few days.'

'And your point is?' Daniel asks, 'Most of the girls I have dated, I have met straight away. Not everyone has a chance to find everything about each other before meeting. If that were the case, you wouldn't need a date because you would have nothing to talk about.'

He is completely right, and after double checking he is okay to babysit, I message Adam and tell him I would love to have a drink.

Annie's Tavern at 9?

I have just over an hour and a half to get ready.

See you then I type back, now the nerves are kicking in.

ANNIE'S TAVERN...

Daniel is in the kitchen when I return from my bedroom all dressed up. I am wearing a figure-hugging dark green dress with lace detail. It is warm outside, so I have a thin black knee-length jacket. I am wearing my hair down, and I have done my makeup with dark green and blended it to give me the Smokey eyes effect to match my dress. I think I look completely different once I make a bit of an effort and I think my brother agrees when he sees me.

'Wow sis, you scrub up well,' he smiles passing me a cigarette he has just made for me, 'Calm your nerves,' he laughs.

'I am feeling the nerves now,' I joke.

'You will be fine once you get a drink in you,' Daniel says as my taxi beeps outside. 'Have fun,' he says.

'Thank you so much, see you later.'

Now that I am in the taxi I am feeling nervous as hell. Adam has already messaged me to say that he is waiting outside for me and will be having a smoke.

My hands have gone clammy as I reach for my purse to pay the taxi driver. I have been to Annie's a few times, so I know where I am going at least.

'That's seven pounds eighty,' the taxi driver says.

I reach forward to give him the exact amount in change, and a little part of me wants to ask the driver just to take me back home, but Adam has just spotted me and waved at me in acknowledgment. I have no choice but to get out of the taxi and I give myself a mental telling off for acting so childish.

Adam greets me with a hug and a small peck on the cheek, and I giggle nervously as his lips tickle my skin. This man is very handsome, and I don't think his photo's do him much justice. I tell him so as well, and I am waiting for him to say something about my photo's which clearly make me look a lot younger than I am.

'Do you really think I look better in real life?' he asks.

'Yes, I do.'

I think I just made him blush a little which is nice to see.

'Anyway Madame, what would you like to drink?' he asks

'A rum and coke please.'

'Do you have any identification?' Adam jokes.

'I do actually,' I smile at him.

'Oh, go on, let me see it,' he teases so I make the mistake of showing him my hideous driving license photo.

'Shit some things should stay hidden, and that is one of them my dear, sorry but that is scary.'

We walk over to the bar, Adam is still chuckling to himself about my photo.

'Hey, it isn't that bad,' I say defending myself.

'If you had that as your profile pic, I might have never spoken to you,' he laughs.

'I am sorry, my one is just as bad, but we have to make it to the second date if you want to see it.'

'That sounds like a dare,' I joke.

'Here, if you can cope with me for more than one evening then fair fucks to you because I can't stand myself the best of times.'

I haven't stopped smiling since I got here, and my face is starting to hurt. Adam is just as funny, if not funnier in person and I like his company so far. We head outside for a smoke and Adam pulls a chair out for me, he also opened the door as we made our way outside.

'A gentleman as well as a funny man,' I say.

'My Granny always said to treat a woman in a gentle fashion but keep her smiling while you do so,' Adam says placing his drink on the table before moving a seat for himself.

'Well I agree with your Gran,' I smile.

Adam and I are talking freely for ages before we decided to head back inside to order another drink. I am finding him easy to talk to. I feel comfortable around him for some reason, and this is a new feeling for me, it doesn't stop my mouth from running away from me though. I over talk when I am nervous, and as much as I try to tame it, I can't ever stop the words from spilling out of me. When I am feeling like this, I talk for the sake of it. Adam doesn't seem to be fazed, and I haven't put him off yet, so all is good. Once inside we make our way over to a table, Adam says he will order us a drink and walks over to the bar. I can feel my cheeks hurting from smiling so much.

When Adam returns to the table my cheeks go bright red.

'Wow,' he says.

I am unsure what he means but guessing it is because I have removed my long black coat and now revealing my new green dress which I have to say was a bargain price from Primark.

'Why thank you,' I say as Adam hands me my drink.

'I really like your attire,' he smiles.

'Believe it or not, this dress cost me less than my drink.'

'Well you wouldn't have guessed, Sarah you look stunning. Can you stand so that I can see you properly?' he asks.

Now it is more than just my face that is on fire. My whole-body temperature has just risen through the roof.

Adam is smiling at me, and this is making me feel more attractive than I think I have ever felt. Wow. One compliment is all it takes to make me feel nervous as hell around him again.

'Trust me, I look better with my clothes on!' I blurt out. There goes my stupid nervous talk again, why did I just say that. I make a rod for my own back, and I know I do.

'I think I should be the judge of that,' Adam jokes.

Oh shit, I hadn't thought that far ahead. This man may see me naked one day, and the thought scares the shit out of me. Adam is a few years younger than me, not that it should matter, but with looking around me all night and seeing how pretty the girls his own age look, how flawless their skin is and how much effort they put into their appearance is intimidating to me. Something tells me that my thirty-odd-year-old body, which has carried children wouldn't be a pretty sight for a young, handsome looking man. I have never been confident about my own body, and just the thought of this going any further is frightening. I have stretch marks covering my stomach, scars from the operations when I was younger and scars from my childhood. Some you can't see, but I know they are there. Damaged goods, Greg once called me, and that's how I am feeling.

Adam can tell I was feeling uncomfortable and has changed the subject, we are now talking about favourite foods, and I warn him I am the fussiest eater he will ever meet. He laughs at me and says that if I become his friend, he will make me try all sorts of new things.

'If you don't try it, you will never know,' he says.

'You do have a point, but I just know what I like and stick to it,' I explain. 'I love meat and a proper Sunday dinner.'

'You love meat?' he says, his eyes widening as a smile appears on his face. Adam's green eyes seem more saturated with colour when he smiles.

Within minutes our harmless conversation about food has turned into a talk about our sexual preferences. By now the rum has started to take control, and I can feel the nervous energy bubbling away inside me, but it doesn't stop my mouth from running away from me. I explain to Adam that I have never really dated in the past and that all my relationships have just sort of developed into something. I tell him that I have only been with a few men and most of which would treat me like a porcelain doll.

'I had a bad upbringing, but that meant the men I was with would be scared to pull my hair even,' I say.

'So, do you like it rough?' Adams smile forms on his face again as he bites down on his bottom lip.

'I wouldn't know Adam. I need to trust the person before I would even attempt anything which you may class as rough, I need to be in control,' I explain.

'Like a sub-dom role?' he asks.

Now I have heard about 50 shades, but I haven't had the time to read the book. I wouldn't know what a sub-dom role is really, but I tell him that I would be far too sweet to be domineering.

'Maybe one day we can test this theory, I don't mind you telling me what to do,' he says before asking if we want to head out for a smoke.

It is almost eleven when Adam tells me that he needs to head home as he has work the next morning.

'Do you fancy a little detour before I drop you off at home?' he asks.

'Well, I guessed I would be getting a taxi home because you have been drinking,' I say.

'I have had two beers all night, I am fine, honestly,' he says, and I believe him.

Adam left most of his last drink on the table, so he has only really had one pint and is under the drink-drive limit. I feel my heart start to race again as I realise I have just agreed to go out in the dark for a drive with a man I have known for only a matter of hours. There is something about Adam though that makes me feel at ease and I have just messaged my brother to tell him what my plan is, just in case. We cannot be too careful nowadays.

We start walking up the street to where Adam has parked his car, well I say his but he has just told me that we can't smoke in the car as it belongs to his Mum and that his own vehicle is in for repairs. As we get towards the car, Adam smiles at me and tells me that he has really enjoyed spending time with me. He opens the passenger door, and I have to say he does come across as the perfect gentleman. I thank Adam as I take my seat.

It is pitch black, and the drive isn't very well lit so I have no idea where he is taking me, but he has me feeling safe enough as he continues to tell me more about himself. We slow down, and I can see an industrial estate in front of us, now I am a little weary and ask why he would bring me here, he explains that this is the road he takes to work and points to a big building in the distance. Adam says that I should feel sorry for him as he will be stuck in there in less than twelve hours. Just as I am about to ask why his workplace would be the ideal place to stop for a smoke, I am hit with the view of the ocean. It looks almost mesmerizing as I watch the moon reflecting off the calm waves.

'Beautiful isn't it?' Adam says seeing the big smile on my face.

I love nature in all its shapes and forms, and Belfast has some amazing views so far. The sea is within touching distance, and the only thing between us is some oversized boulders of blackened rock.

Once we both get out of the car I look up at the cloudless, sparkling night sky while Adam starts to walk over to the large rocks, he climbs up making it look easy and turns back around to face me.

'You should come and stand up here,' he shouts just as the wind picks up in my ears.

I just laugh and shake my head at him in disbelief.

'I can't swim Adam, so you wouldn't ever catch me up there,' I confessed. I think he is slightly shocked or amused.

'Honestly, you never learnt how to swim?' he asks in a slightly sarcastic tone, now I can tell he is a little amused.

I shake my head at him feeling slightly embarrassed.

'There seems to be a lot of things you have never done,' he says shouting back over to me.

It is getting cold and my thin jacket is doing nothing to keep that sea breeze off me.

Once Adam returns over to the front of the car where I am still standing, he must have noticed that I am cold and offers to put his arms around me.

Adam then lights up his pre-rolled cigarette and puts his arms around me using his jacket to shield me from the wind that is now picking up with some extra force.

I wouldn't normally like being hugged but I feel relaxed in his hold. I smile to myself as Adam passes me the smoke because it is strange that I feel like I have known this man for a while, even though we only met properly a few hours ago. I am feeling a little disappointed as I feel the cold hit me as soon as Adam has let go of me. I think I am feeling deflated as he moves out of the way and starts to walk back around the car.

I thought he was going to kiss me when I felt his mouth close to my neck, but I am guessing he is too much of a gentleman to kiss me without checking first.

'I will take you home so that you can get warmed up,' he says opening the passenger door for me.

As much as I am gutted that he hasn't made a move on me or anything I know that I can't let anything happen on the first night, what would the man think of me?

I cannot lie and say that I wasn't hoping for a kiss because since our conversation heated up, so did my imagination.

The drive home is quiet, so I am left to my own thoughts, and I am half wondering why has Adam gone so quiet now, he has been very chatty up to now. I am starting to wonder if I have said something wrong, though I can't recall saying anything that would put him off me.

Well, I don't think I did anyway.

As we arrive outside my house, there is a little awkward moment as I undo my seatbelt.

I think about leaning in for a thank you kiss on his cheek but am a little worried he will turn me down, and I don't want to look foolish, so I just smile at him and bid him a good night. Adam says he will message me tomorrow and I hope he does.

EMOTIONAL BLACKMAIL…

Recently I have had a lot of guilt hidden inside me, first of all, because Adam and I are getting on so well. We have been on a few dates now and even though we have both said we don't want anything serious I can feel myself liking him too much as well. I am starting to move on, and I know Stuart has only been dead a year, but Adam is the nicest man I have ever met. Am I moving on too soon? Since Father's Day, I have felt a little bit of hatred towards Stuart. The more and more I think about that woman messaging me the more annoyed I am getting. I know deep down that the man must have loved me, but now I feel like my marriage was a joke to him. Stuart spent a lot of time out on the road at the beginning of our relationship, and I never imagined at the time that he would even consider cheating on me, but he did. Stuart would jump at the chance to travel long distance runs at work, and the more I think about it, he never seemed to get an extra wage for all the driving he was doing. It is starting to make a little sense now, but I will never know. I will never be able to ask him which just makes this even harder.

I really like spending time with Adam, but I am wondering if my anger blinds me. The anger I feel towards my cheating dead husband or if I like Adam for who he is. Adam and I have spoken a lot, and I have even gone as far to tell him the outline of my childhood. Part of me was hoping I would scare the man away, but Adam didn't have it easy himself. He was never abused or anything, but he still had his own story to tell. Both Lucy and Harry have met him as well, just because we have been seeing each other for a few weeks now and with me being a single mother, it is easier to see him at my place in the evenings and weekends.

I have also been getting a lot of messages off Rachel and Carl the past few weeks. They are both saying the same thing, but Rachel is a more polite in her approach. Neither of them believes that their Dad cheated on me for so long, and they are trying to convince me that it is all lies. Carl says I am nasty for even thinking his Dad would do such a thing, and both are asking me to return home. Carl has gone as far to say that he will ring social services on me if I don't at least think about returning home.

It is my own doing because I was on Facebook badmouthing their Father a little. I was basically saying that I cannot trust anyone, not even my cheating Husband but I do understand why that has upset Stuart's children. It wasn't nice to read, and I should have kept that private.

That post has also made my cousin Katie message me. I hadn't spoken to her properly for a while and the last time I did see her was at Stuart's funeral. It was a little awkward as we hadn't spoken before that for almost ten years. Katie has been my vent, and I have been messaging her about this whole situation. When I told her about Carl's threat, she says that she half agrees with him, not that I should have made a phone call but that I do need the support of my family and that I have been cruel to take Harry and Lucy away from their siblings.

So, as you can imagine the guilt is eating me up lately.

It hasn't gone unnoticed and my Mum has called in to check that I am okay.

'It is emotional blackmail, don't listen to them,' she says, but it isn't my mother who keeps getting the messages.

'I am trying, but I can kind of see where they are coming from,' I sigh.

'Look, Sarah, if Stu did cheat, which I am sorry to say this, but it wouldn't surprise me in the slightest. Then you owe his children nothing, as harsh as that sounds but it is true.'

Mum was right and I try and put all this stress behind me.

'All this crying makes me look ugly,' I say.

'You never look ugly you dick,' Mum laughs.

Adam is due around tonight, and I want to have a bath and make a little bit of effort for him. Mum has offered to have my children over night, so we have the option to go out if we want to.

'Thank you Mummy,' I say in my sweetest voice.

'Just be at my house early to collect them, I can't be doing with arguing kids all day,' she says.

Adam and I head out to a small pub close to where he lives. The evening is going well, but I am surprised when he informs me that he needs to drop me off at home earlier than expected. He says he has work stupidly early and that his head is killing him, so by ten o clock I am in bed, on my own. Adam tells me that he will see me tomorrow evening instead and kisses me in the car before driving off down the road. I am feeling frustrated and annoyed, but I am sure he is sincere, and he did look like the light was hurting his eyes. I message my Mum to tell her that I am home already and head straight to bed.

My phone beeps, and I guess it must be my Mother wanting to know why we were only out an hour, but it is Adam wishing me a goodnight and apologising for cutting our evening short.

As soon as I wake up, I send Adam a good morning message. It is almost seven in the evening when I hear back from Adam. He is saying that he has been flat out at work today and has asked if he can come and see me tomorrow evening instead. I agree, but I am left worrying that he is going off me already. His messages are short and to the point, instead of his usual flirty messages and no kisses on the end.

Now I am pissed off but more so at myself for feeling like this. We have both said that this is nothing serious and more like two good friends enjoying each other's company. Feelings shouldn't come into it, but I am feeling a lot of emotions lately, and I don't like it.

FEELING ALONE AGAIN…

It has been a lovely day today, the sun has been beaming down, and the kids have been in such a good mood. We went to the museum followed by lunch in town and neither of them argued which is a blessing lately. Harry is still refusing to sleep in a different room to his sister, so we have a spare room to play about with. At the minute we have a dart board in there for when my brother comes to visit, but I haven't seen him in a few days. I am in a bit of a huff with my Mum at the moment, so I haven't been over to see her in about a week. I am still having a few problems with my neighbour and my Mother knows the woman because she used to live in the same hostel as her, yet she refuses to back my corner. The woman keeps targeting my house, and she stands outside with all the young teenage lads giving them eggs to throw at my door. All this just because Harry had thrown a stone which ended up hitting her daughter. I would be angry too, but my son was disciplined, and I don't know what else she is expecting from me. My Mum knows I am annoyed with her too. I am guessing that is why she hasn't been to see me either.

As soon as we are home the kids go over to the park to play. I don't have any housework to do, and we have only just eaten, so I decide it is a brilliant idea to paint a big tunnel on the wall, for Harry and I plan to paint a princess castle for Lucy. Both the kids love playing with chalk, and because one of the other tenants complained about having a coloured in driveway, I have had to ask my kids to keep the chalk indoors. I plan to use blackboard paint on the inside of the painting, so my children can still play with their beloved chalk.

About an hour and a half worth of painting and I am interrupted by a knock on the door.

It's Adam.

'Oh hello, I wasn't expecting you until later,' I say surprised that he didn't message to say he was on his way over.

'Sorry beautiful, I was going to message, but I thought I would surprise you instead. Am I interrupting you?' he asks.

'Not at all, come in. I just need to wash my hands,'

I make my way to the spare room and close the lids to my paint. I pick up my brushes. I may as well wash them while I do my hands.

When I return to the living room, Adam has made himself comfortable on the sofa. I had already turned the kettle on before coming up the hall.

'Tea or coffee?' I ask.

'Can't I just have you?' Adam jokes, and I just raise my eyebrow at him, 'Tea please.'

I am smiling like a stupid giddy teenager as I prepare our hot drinks, but Adam was about to take the stupid smile back off my face.

When I sit down beside him, he doesn't cuddle into me like he has when we have been on our own lately. Instead, he asks me if I can budge up the sofa a little so that he can stretch his legs. I am trying not to show it, but I am a little upset. Adam seems off today, and something tells me I have said or done something to annoy him.

'What's up?' I finally ask.

'Nothing, my head is just fried with everything lately,' he says, 'I am in good need of a holiday I think.'

I would love a holiday I think to myself, 'I have only ever been aboard once.'

'Yes, you said,' his voice is a little short.

'Maybe I can cheer you up?' I tease.

'Sarah, sex isn't the answer!' he snaps.

'I am sorry, but my head is starting to get fucked, and I think I need some space,' he finally says.

'Oh,' I say not expecting those words to come out of his mouth.

'I know I am a bastard, but we did always say that this was never going to be anything serious,' Adam places his hand on my leg and he tries to look me in the eyes, but I turn my head away.

'So, are you saying goodbye then?' I ask trying to hide my hurt.

'I am saying a bye for now,' he attempts to hold my hand, 'Sarah I really like you, but I am not ready for all this complicated mess. I don't want to hurt you.'

Too late for that I want to say, but instead, I tell him that I understand. I am only hurting because I have let myself start to like this man too much. Adam made me feel comfortable from the very start, and we may not have been seeing each other for long but I still felt close to him, and I know I am going to miss him.

'You know I can't promise I will still be single when you decide you want me again,' I say quite bluntly.

'I know Sarah, you are a beautiful woman with a kind heart, I cannot imagine you being single for long, but that is a chance I am willing to make.'

'Cheers,' I say.

'I told you from the start I am not the type of man you pin your hopes on, and you agreed that we would keep each other at arms-length.'

Adam is right, and I am glad that he is putting an end to this now, rather than a few months down the line. If this is how hurt I am feeling now, then God knows how upset I would have been if he left it too long to tell me.

'Does arm's length mean we can't be friends either?' I ask.

'Don't be silly. We can be friends, but just not this type of friends,' he says pulling me in for a cuddle.

'I am sorry Sarah,' he whispers kissing me on the forehead.

'So am I.'

Adam goes home after he has finished his cup of tea and told me that he would speak to me again in a few weeks. I want to believe him, but I don't, and I end up breaking down into tears as soon as I close my front door.

My week doesn't seem to get any better either when another run-in with my neighbour ends with a tub of paint being thrown at my front door. Lucy and Harry were watching a DVD when it happened, and it scared the life out of them.

'Is this because Harry was naughty Mum?' Lucy asks.

'Partly,' I explain, 'Harry throwing the stone may have started all this, but it is that lady across the street that is causing all this, not you kids.'

Harry is far from an angel lately, but my kids have been through a lot, and I am not one of these parents who will sugar-coat everything and ignore a child's unruly behaviour, but at the time I punished Harry and removed all treats and technology for a week. Harry has been punished so that should be the end of it.

Katie has been messaging me all morning, so of course, I tell her about my crazed neighbour. Katie thinks I should go back home for a few weeks to get away from it all and I am starting to think that it isn't such a bad idea after all. At least I will be away from all the street wars.

I am talking to my Mother again, after realising that she won't ever back my corner. I decided to either let it bother me or just ignore it, and I choose the latter option. After talking with Katie and calling my kids from the playroom, I head over to my Mums with the plan to tell her I am going away for a bit. My Mum has Daniel living with her now, so I know she won't be lonely with me gone.

Mum seems a little more upset than I anticipated.

'Are you going then and what is your plan?' she asks

'Well I have spoken with Katie, and she has said I could go over and stay with her whenever I want. Mum, I need to sort my head out,' I explain.

'When are you going?' she sounds upset.

'As soon as I can afford our tickets, Belfast hasn't been what I expected so far what with the neighbours and now Adam,'

'You haven't given it time and running away isn't the answer,' she snaps.

I know she is right, but running away is what I do best, even if I hate admitting, that this is what I do.

'I am not running away. I am just getting away to clear my head,' I feel like I have to defend myself a little and I am only going for a break.

'Will you be back?' her voice sound cracked as if she is about to cry.

'Yes Mum, of course I will be back,' I say this, but I have no idea what I am doing really.

I am hoping a little time back home will make me figure out what is best. The kids have both said they don't care where we live but all this moving about isn't good for them either.

BACK HOME FOR A WHILE...

Mum has offered to put my kids and I up for a few days until I have the money for our boat home. I am not looking forward to the ten-hour travelling with the kids, but it is the cheapest option. I have messaged Stuart's kids to tell them that I will be back home for a while and I have asked them to come to my cousin's house and see us. Katie has informed me that she has organized a family get together for my return even though I asked her not to make a fuss. I haven't seen half of my aunts or cousins in years, so I know it will be awkward and that is the last thing I need at the minute, but when Katie gets an idea in her head she runs with it. I think she is more excited to have me back than anything else. It is nice to feel wanted.

I have packed as little as possible because I am planning on coming back. My ticket is an open return too, I have a month to sort my head out. Luckily, I have my rent paid directly to the landlord, so Andrew shouldn't know I am even gone. Mum has agreed to open and close my curtains, and I have a man coming to the flat tomorrow afternoon to repaint the window ledge for me. I have managed to scrub most of the paint from my windows, and I am just grateful the neighbours didn't see me while I was doing so. Mum has said I am a dick for going back, but she won't change my mind. The kids have been told that we are going back for a while and Harry is excited to see his big brother, so nothing my Mum says is going to change my mind.

The kids were bored silly on the train, but now we are on the boat they seem to have perked up. We ended up getting on the night boat because I was hoping they would both sleep the eight-hour journey but instead they are full of beans and chasing each other around the play area. No doubt one of them will be over to me within minutes crying. That is what usually happens when they are overtired.

I could sleep myself, but it doesn't look like it is going to happen, so I decide to turn on my data and check on my Facebook to keep me awake. I am scrolling through and can see a post off Katie saying that she feels like she is getting her baby cousin back and that she can't wait. I comment on her post that I cannot wait to see her either and continue to scroll down my newsfeed. Then I come across a post off Adam. I had almost forgotten that I added him on Facebook as he is never online and never usually puts up a post. By the looks of things, he managed to get that holiday he had been wanting and had tagged a girl in his post with him. That makes me want to open the post and look through all twenty-nine photos. Adam looks happy, and the scenery around him is to die for. I am reminded of the way he looked that first time I met him. Those big green eyes of his twinkling while he smiled. Adam hasn't been in contact with me for over a month now, and I am guessing by these pictures that he hasn't taken a second to think about me. Whoever the girl is in these photo's they are both very close and that makes me feel jealous and annoyed. I know I have no right to feel this way and we did say that we weren't an item but looking at these photographs and seeing how happy he is looking makes me feel a little used. If he had stayed in touch like he said he would, then maybe I wouldn't feel so betrayed, but Adam knew my biggest secret and helped me not to feel ashamed of my past. He made me feel wanted and even though we said we wouldn't gain feelings, he did make me think that he was just as into me as I was with him. I honestly thought he would be different to everyone else, but I must have been mistaken. I go to his profile and block him. I don't need someone who can just walk away like that, part of my life. I have lost enough as it is.

We arrive at my cousin's house just before dinner time the next day. Katie is all giggly and introduces herself to Harry and Lucy as Aunt Kate. She has gone to a lot of trouble making sandwiches and nibbles and I slightly offended when I tell her that I am not hungry.

'You will eat young lady,' she snaps.

Lucy sniggers because her Mum has clearly been told off.

'And don't you giggle, or you will be sent upstairs,' Katie tells Lucy sternly.

'I think we should do as we are told,' I joke to Lucy, so she knows that Katie is only playing with her.

We sit down, and I nibble on my sandwich while Harry takes the ham and cheese from inside his bread to eat it separately.

'I hope you are not playing with your food young man?' my cousin pipes up, 'Oh, I am only joking,' she says as Harry's eyes fill with tears.

I calm my son down and get him to eat his filling at least, 'He doesn't eat bread lately,' I explain to Katie who is shaking her head at me.

'He's a fussy nuisance like his Mother then.'

I know Katie is just trying to be funny, but after travelling all night, I am exhausted and ready to drop and tell her how wrecked I am feeling.

'Go up and have a shower to wake up,' she says.

I was hoping she would offer to watch my kids while I got my head down for an hour, but I suppose she doesn't know them so wouldn't want sole responsibility for them on the first day of meeting them. I am in and out of the shower as quickly as I can, more so because I need to sit down and don't want to leave the kids downstairs with Katie for too long.

When I return down the stairs, I meet Katie's eldest son Mitch.

'I knew you when you were a baby,' I say looking at this tall teenage boy standing in front of me.

'She's right,' Katie says as her son looks over at her, 'Your Auntie Sarah lived with us for a while, and she used to visit when you and your bother were both little.'

I nod my head in agreement.

'How long is she staying?' Mitch asks as if I am not in the room.

'As long as she needs to, now go back to your room before I get annoyed with you again.'

'Sorry Sarah but he has been under my feet all week, the little shit got suspended for a week and is doing my head in,' Katie says to explain why she has just snapped at her son.

'You don't need to explain anything to me.'

We settle into Katie's house that evening with ease. The fact that my two are shattered from all the traveling has helped so by nine in the evening Katie, and I are on our own chatting in the kitchen. The conversation is mainly about my crazed neighbour, but then she asks me about the lad I was seeing.

'We weren't really together,' I explain.

'So, it was just sex?' she asks me rather bluntly.

'Well no not really.'

'Not really, it either was, or it wasn't!' she snaps.

'We were what you call friends with benefits,' I joke.

'So, the man was using you for sex then!' she states.

I am a little unsure why she is so blunt with me, she was fine a few moments ago, and as soon as our conversation turns to my love life, she is snappy and being quite rude to me. I have never been with anyone for just sex and as much as Adam and I agreed that it was a no strings relationship. Katie has left me feeling dirty and used.

'You are too old for just sex,' she says.

'Thanks,' I say as I take offense to what she has just said.

'I am in my thirties and old enough to make my own mistakes,' I said defending myself.

'Well don't think you will be making any stupid mistakes while you are under my roof,' she tries to talk in a calmer tone, but it fails.

'I wasn't planning on doing anything while I am here.'

The way she is talking to me makes me wonder why I even travelled back home in the first place, at least in Belfast I didn't have anyone talking down to me like an unruly teenager. I want to tell her to stop talking to me like shit, but I am in her house, so I need to respect her rules. Not that I would have even thought about meeting up with another man, not anytime soon anyway.

'Right I am going to bed, you are in with me,' she says getting to her feet, 'Well come on then.'

Is she really sending me up to bed at half past nine? I know I am sharing a room with her, but I didn't expect to be told a bedtime. As I have said, this is her home, so I can't really argue but what a way to make me feel untrusted. I would happily stay awake until midnight at least, and I know I will not be able to sleep this early, but I grab my bag and follow my cousin up to her room. I place my belongings on the floor by her wardrobe and check on my kids who are in the room next to us fast asleep. I am grateful that Katie has given my children their own room while we are here, but I am wishing I could just climb into a single bed with my children instead of sleeping in the same room as Katie. I bite my tongue when she tells me to hurry up and turn the light off.

'We wake up at six in this house,' she says as she turns over and wishes me a good night sleep.

Six?? I haven't been awake that early in a long time, but I cannot argue with her rules.

'Fucks sake!' Katie mutters as my phone starts to beep.

'Sorry,' I placed my phone on silent.

I decide to check it in the morning when I am expected to wake up as early as the birds.

'Goodnight,' I say as I roll over onto my side.

OLD MEMORIES…

Living back at my cousins is not what I had expected it to be like. Katie comes across as quite
mean and, dare is say spiteful, even my children
have said she is a scary villain that you would find
in a movie. Cruella DeVille comes to mind. Katie
and I almost argued the other day. She had told
Lucy off for saying no to me. I was dealing with my
daughter when Katie jumped in and started
screaming at Lucy for her apparent lack of respect
towards me, her Mother. I tried to tell Katie that
Lucy was my responsibility and that I would sort
her out, but I was told that while we were under
her roof, we were all to do as we were told, including me. I was sent out of the room while my daughter was told to sit on the stairs for an hour and not
move.

As soon as the hour was up, my children and I
went out to visit my brother Callum. He is Daniel's
twin, but I hadn't seen him for over thirteen years.
We had spoken a few times briefly when Stuart
died and if I had seen him at our Mum's in passing,
but Callum and I didn't know each other, and I be-

lieved it was time to make that effort. I had been told that he wouldn't talk to me before, as he has spent most of our lives living with our Father. When my parents split up, Callum went with him, while Daniel stayed with our Mother.

Callum had messaged me while I was in Belfast telling me that it was about time we both put the past behind us. I have never spoken to him about my past, but he means the fact that I had apparently told lots of lies when we were younger and that it was me who caused our Father to run away. I let Callum believe what he wants because in all honesty, I am sick and tired of even defending myself anymore. There really is no point.

It was a little awkward at my brother's house, I felt like I was a stranger, but I am sure it will get a little easier as time goes on. Within an hour I had headed back to Katie's house.

I decide to message my brother and ask if he minds us visiting again today and he replied saying it would be nice to see us. The kids have been pains getting ready, but we finally leave the house just after two in the afternoon. It is a warm day, so we have taken a slow walk to my brother's house. Callum opens his door and offers me a coffee and the kids a drink of juice.

'Thank you,' I say as he passes the kids a carton of juice each.

I am here less than an hour when Katie rings me to tell me that I am due home for my dinner. I explain that I am at Callum's house and that we have not long got here. I was expecting her to understand after not speaking to her own siblings in years herself, but Katie just tells me that I have half an hour to get home. Otherwise, our dinner will be put in the bin.

'Is she being fucking serious?' Callum asks when I tell him about my phone call.

'Apparently so,' I joke.

Katie is not the person I remember when we were teenagers, life seems to have toughened her up admittedly but there really is no need to be nasty. I haven't had it easy myself so people who say they are bitches because men have made them that way I lose all respect for. Something I taught myself from such a young age is that I have control of the way I deal with something. At times in my life, that was the only form of control or freedom I had. Blaming others for the way we act is the biggest cop-out of them all.

'Why is she such a bitch?' Ally asks

Ally is Callum's long term girlfriend.

'Life apparently,' I say as I gather my belongings from the kitchen table.

'Don't tell me you are actually going?' My brother asks, sounding a little annoyed.

'If I don't go now, she will be in a mood with us all evening, and that isn't fair on the kids,' I explain.

'Fuck her, you can stay here for a few days,' he says.

As much as it is a nice offer, I really do not want to intrude on my brother who I have only just started speaking to. So, I decline but promise that I will be back to visit very soon.

'That's if she doesn't ground you,' he jokes as my brother and his missus walk me to the door.

'See you on Saturday,' I say.

'See you Saturday, bye kids,' Callum says.

Lucy shouts back, but Harry hasn't spoken. To be fair Harry hasn't talked much all day.

CONFUSED AND USED...

I had been staying with Katie for too long now, and I needed to get out of her house. We hadn't argued as such, but the woman was trying to control me more than my late Husband had, and I was ready to snap. My brother Callum had mentioned that the landlord had an empty house available and that he had put my name forward for it. Luckily, I was given the tenancy and moved out of my cousin's house a few days later. Katie said she was sad to see me go, but I could tell my kids were happy to leave, which I think added to my own feelings as well.

The house I have now is small, but it will do the job for now. I wasn't even planning on getting a house back here, and it all seemed to happen quicker than I have been able to process, and now I have the awkward conversation with my Mum about how I am staying here for six months at least. My landlord is a sleazy Indian man who keeps looking me up and down when he talks to me, and it is making me feel a little uncomfortable. Callum says he will have a word with Mr. Sharma on my behalf.

It is Halloween tomorrow, and I have been sewing fabric together to make Lucy's witch outfit. She didn't like any of the shop bought dresses, so I told her I would try and make one for her. I think she deliberately found fault in the stores chosen styles just so that I would make her something unique. I don't mind in the slightest, and it is nice to have something creative to do. Callum has invited the kids and me to his for a Halloween party, and we have also been invited to Katie's house as well. The fact that Callum and I have a lot more in common and he is very down to earth from what I have seen so far, I think we will be heading to his over my cousin's. Katie has our Aunts turning up, and as much as they are all very nice people, I don't really know any of them, and I haven't spent much time with them since I lived at home with that monster and my Mum. The same can be said about Callum, but he is my brother so in my head has a little more right to my loyalty. Katie hasn't said anything directly to me, but I have been told that she is slagging me off behind my back to some of our other cousins, saying that I have used her. I feel bad that she thinks that way, but living with her was not easy, and I have just taken a small back step from her, until she calms down.

It is getting late, so I decide to head to bed, but I check on the time on my mobile, thinking it must be at least midnight. I am surprised when I see it is closer to four in the morning.

'Christ, I have to be up in three hours,' I mutter to myself.

I hear my alarm going off, but I am sure that I have only just drifted to sleep so I set it to snooze, or so I thought I did. When I was finally woken by Harry, it was past ten in the morning. Luckily the kids haven't started school yet. Otherwise, I would have been late. They start after the half term which means I can try sorting our lives out while they are in school all day. A part-time job working from ten till two would be ideal, but I cannot see it happening somehow.

Lucy is excited as I head down the stairs with her dress that I was awake half the night making. I don't know what her mood is about this morning, but she has told me that it isn't as nice as she imagined.

'I am creative, but there is only so much I can do with my bare hands,' I say.

'Well I have to wear it now,' she sulks.

This is all I need today, so I try and reason with my daughter, but she is having none of it. I have ruined her Halloween seemingly.

'I cannot win lately,' I mutter as I make my way into the kitchen to make my morning cup of tea.

'Lucy!' I shout as soon as I witness the state of my kitchen sides.

'What!' she walks into the kitchen still sulking over her dress that I am quite proud of.

'How many times do I have to ask you to clean up after yourself,' I ask.

'It was Harry,' she says.

Harry denies even being in the kitchen as Lucy starts shouting at him that he is a liar.

'Enough!' I shout after listening to them bicker long enough.

'Mum, I didn't even come into the kitchen,' Harry pleads with me.

'Whatever,' Lucy mutters.

I know my eleven year old daughter well enough to know that when she says, 'Whatever,' it usually means that she knows she is in the wrong. For some reason lately, she keeps trying to blame her little brother for everything and refusing to take responsibility no matter whether she has been caught red-handed or not. I really wish my daughter would be a bit more helpful.

Most of the day Lucy was moping about the house with a face like thunder. I really do not know what has gotten into her. I decide a little pampering session before we start getting our Halloween costumes on, might cheer her up, so I start to run her a bath and plan to paint her nails and curl her hair. She usually would like that.

The pampering session seemed to work a little, and now that her witches dress is on, she is saying she loves it. I think she just woke up on the wrong side of the bed. I have spoken to my brother and asked who will be at his house this evening, and I am a little taken back when he starts to list off loads of names. The thought of going to his house and not knowing anyone is a little intimidating for me, but I know I must do something. I had spoken to my Mother earlier, and she seems very happy that Callum and I are now on talking terms, but she has warned that if I don't show up tonight, that it could be enough for my brother to stop talking to me again. Feeling uncomfortable and already warned I decided to have a little drink before I start the ten-minute walk to Callum's.

Katie has messaged to say that the whole family was hoping to see me, and I feel a little bad that I told her I couldn't make it tonight. She has taken offense that I would rather go to see my brother tonight, than go to her house.

'Please don't say we have to go to Aunty Katie's,' Harry says.

'No son, we don't.'

'That's good because I know it is Halloween, but she is scary,' he says all matter of a fact.

'You make me smile Harry,' Lucy says agreeing with her little brother.

'We are going to my brother's house,' I explain as we head out of the door.

HALLOW'S EVE...

It is just past eight in the evening, the kids are settled in the living room with a DVD and some of their treats from this evenings trick or treating, and I am feeling a little worse for wear. It doesn't help that I hadn't eaten earlier, and Callum has been very forceful while pouring our drinks. I am told that Barry is turning up any minute and Callum's friend Nathan is on his way too. Callum is making a point of telling me that they are both single.

'Barry as in Dad's old mate?' I asked surprised that my brother still talks to him.

'Yeah, shit I forget you used to live with us,' he laughs 'Barry is alright.'

'Just so that you know I am not interested in meeting anyone,' I explain.

Ally looks at me and says she doesn't blame me 'Men are twats,' she smiles.

I don't know what it is but seeing Barry in front of me has made me feel uncomfortable, I remember him always sitting around the table with my Dad smoking weed and sharing a crack pipe. He looks like he has sorted his life out a bit with his appearance at least, but the man just reminds me of my Father. Then he makes me feel worse by asking if I have heard from my Dad lately.

'Not since he moved away,' I say, my voice cracking at the mere mention of his name.

'He's back. I hear,' Barry smiles.

Did he just say my Dad is back in Crosby?

'I wouldn't know, I don't speak to him.'

'It's a shame, Sarah, he isn't the man we used to know,' Callum says defending the vile man.

'That's good to hear but none of my business.'

Well that conversation killed the atmosphere, I know it is Halloween but come on. Callum has started having a big talk with Barry about my Dad, so I make my excuses and go in the other room to check on the kids. They are both fast asleep on the sofa and Lucy is cuddling her little brother. This isn't a sight I see often. I am stood in the doorway silently watching my children looking peaceful and angelic when I am startled.

'Sorry I didn't mean to frighten you,' he says.

'It is okay,' I whisper not wanting to wake the kids, 'You must be Nathan?'

'Yes, your brother has told me loads about you,' he smiles, 'you look way better in real life than on the photo's he showed me.'

'Photo's?' I ask feeling slightly amused that Callum has gone to so much effort with his friend.

'Yeah, well he let me scroll through your Facebook photo's,' he says.

Nathan and I go outside for a smoke, and it transpires that he is in the process of leaving his wife.

He is making her sound like she is part of the Russian mafia which is his portrail of his other half.

'Why are you with her then?' I asked wondering why he would put up with the things he is telling me.

'Because we have a daughter together, here look,' he says reaching into his pocket and showing me a photo.

The little girl is beautiful, and I am guessing she is less than a year old. Nathan tells me that his wife has threatened to move away with their fourteen-month-old daughter if he ever leaves her.

'Do you think she will follow through with her threat?' I ask.

Just then my brother and Barry come outside to join us for a smoke break.

'You two look cosy,' Barry mocks.

'We are just talking,' I snap.

I don't like Barry, even though he hasn't done anything to me, I just don't think he is the type of man I could ever get along with. He reminds me too much of my Father.

'He is single Sarah,' Callum says joking with Barry.

'No, he isn't, like I said, we have been talking and I know he has a wife and baby,' I smile smugly at my brother.

'I told you not to tell her,' he hisses at his mate.

'I am not going to lie mate. Your sister seems like a cool girl,' Nathan flashes me a cheeky grin.

'A cool girl, don't make me choke on my smoke,' Callum sniggers.

'I feel like this is taking the piss out of Sarah tonight' I say.

Being in the garden laughing with the men is a little weird to me, I know Callum is my brother, but I don't know him, and him talking about me like he does know me is a little annoying, but I don't say anything. Instead, I keep sipping my drink.

When we head back into the kitchen, Callum asks if we want to have a game of poker. I agree knowing that we used to play the games as kids, and I remembered all the rules. Barry also knew how to play poker as he used to always play the game with my Dad and his mates around our kitchen table when I still lived at home. Nathan was a little worried about playing the games, as he didn't have much money on him as it was.

'The missus only gives me twenty pounds pocket money a week,' he says which I take as a joke.

'I will sub you,' Callum suggests, and Nathan agrees.

We are playing for just over an hour, and it is between my brother and me on who will take the pot home. The bet is up at fifty pounds with ten of that being mine. I'd happily head home forty pounds heavier tonight.

We are sweating it out, and it is down to our last two cards. Callum turns his card first, and he has the jack of hearts.

'Great,' I mutter.

'Can't see you getting higher than that,' Ally says standing behind her boyfriend.

Callum looks up at her and smiles as she kisses him on the head. It is nice to see my brother settled down.

As the evening progresses and the drinks are flowing, I am starting to ease up and enjoying myself. We are playing beer pong when I realize the alcohol is beginning to take effect. I tell my brother that I am going to wake my kids up and ring a taxi, but Ally assures me that I won't get a taxi for a few hours as everyone will be out, it is a Saturday night after all.

'Looks like we are walking then,' I say.

'Leave the kids here if you want to, they will be okay until the morning, and I can just ring you in the morning,' she says.

'Are you sure?' I ask, not sure what is best.

'Yeah, I would have said you could stay too but Barry is in the spare room and your kids are on the sofa.'

'It's okay I will wake them,' I say stumbling into the door frame.

Maybe waking my children from their peaceful sleep while I am slightly drunk isn't the best move I can make as a Mother, so I listen to Ally and decide they can sleep where they are for now.

'I don't want to leave them,' I say as I am almost escorted to the door. Callum and Nathan are outside and offering to walk me the ten minutes to my house.

'Thank you.'

STUPID MISTAKES, LASTING EFFECT...

I am not going to make any excuses for myself, last night I let my brother talk me into offering Nathan a room for the night. He was initially going to be spending the evening on my brother's sofa, but with my children both asleep on them, I felt like I had no choice when Callum asked me to do him a favour. I was annoyed when I realised that I would have woken my children up. The way my brother was laughing at the situation did have me wonder if it was all part of his scheming plan. Callum was always known as the sly twin growing up, whereas Daniel was still as misbehaved but did it in your face.

Now letting the man stay overnight was fine, it was the fact that we continued drinking and then ended up sleeping together that evening that was the stupid mistake. I know Nathan has a wife, and I still let myself get talked into sleeping with him and that fact that should have kept me as far away from him as possible. I have been cheated on and would never have wished it on anyone else, but in my defence, Nathan has spent the whole night telling me how nasty she was to him and even went as far to say that he has had to ring the police on her for attacking him in public. She really does sound like an evil woman and not someone I should be getting involved with. Sleeping with her husband was never my intention, and now I am feeling riddled with guilt.

'You seem quiet,' Nathan says as we are standing awkwardly in my kitchen. The morning after the night before.

I need to go and collect my children, but I feel like I have a neon sign above my head saying I have slept with a married man. I feel so ashamed of my actions that I just want to get this day over and done with.

'I am sorry about last night,' I say quietly into my cup.

'Do not say sorry at all, Sarah you are amazing, and you were amazing,' he smiles, but that just sends a shiver down my spine.

'You're married,' I remind him.

'Yes, to a husband beating, money grabbing cow who doesn't deserve me.'

'Even so,' I sigh, 'You are still married.'

'Please don't keep on reminding me,' he laughs, but I am not in a laughing mood.

Nathan then tries to hug me, but I push him away. 'Please don't, I feel shit enough as it is,' I say.

'Don't, you made me realise that I don't need to stay with that abusing woman,' he says.

'I am glad I have helped somehow, but I still feel like crap.'

I look at him and can feel myself becoming more and more annoyed at myself, 'Come on, I best get my kids, drink up.'

The walk to my brother house is a little awkward. Nathan tries to hold my hand, but I shrug him away.

'Look last night shouldn't have happened,' I snap.

'We can pretend for a few more minutes at least.'

He says, but I tell him that I can't and won't let my children get confused with him acting like we are something that we are not.

'Okay, I get that.'

The situation gets awkward when I get to my brother's house, Ally and Callum are stood outside having a cigarette. I am guessing Nathan had text Callum and informed him of last night as he starts to snigger at us approaching. The problem is that I was so drunk I can barely remember any of last night, and it transpires that Callum and Ally know the whole story.

'I was very drunk and stupid,' I confess to Ally when the men walk in through the front door leaving us to chat, 'I can't even remember sleeping with him, but I know we did.'

'He couldn't have been that good if you can't remember,' she jokes.

'I feel ashamed,' I sigh.

'Don't be silly, you have done nothing wrong, but Nathan has,' she says, but that doesn't make me feel any better.

'Katarina is a crazed bitch, and I am hoping this will give him the push to leave her. Cal agreed with me too and was hoping you would both hit it off.'

'Really, why?' I ask.

'Cal doesn't get to see Nathan usually because since he got with her,' Ally scrunches up her face 'Nathan has been withdrawn and never normally allowed out. He is only here now because she is away visiting family in Russia.'

'Well I don't need the added stress that is sure to come from sleeping with a married man,'

I am shitting myself a little now. No one has painted a good picture of this woman, and I am sure she would eat me alive and spit me out when she finds out.

'You are not in the wrong. He is' Ally repeats herself.

'Plus, she will never find out, I am sure Nathan does this a lot while she is away.'

'Well, that doesn't make me feel any better,' My opinion on myself is at rock bottom and I feel sick, either from shame or the lack of food and a hangover from hell.

'Let's go in. Your kids are watching SpongeBob in the living room.'

'Thank you,' I say.

I peer my head around the doorway and Harry noticed me straight away and ran up to me to hug me. His head collides with my stomach making me feel nauseous again.

'Did you miss me?' I ask.

'Erm sort of,' he smiles.

After I have sat down and had my brother take the piss out of me constantly for an hour, I am finally ready to go home and feel sorry for myself. It is the walk home when my daughter asks if we can go to the park that I decide I will try and put my shameful antics behind me and enjoy my Sunday morning with my children.

We decide to have dinner out so after we are all bathed and changed into smarter clothes I ring our taxi.

'Do you want to go to the cinema?' I ask still feeling guilty for leaving them with my brother overnight.

'Can we have popcorn?' Lucy grins.

'Only if you eat all your dinner,' I reply.

That afternoon I can honestly say had been the best day in a long time. Spending quality time with my children made me appreciate their company even more. I think it has finally dawned on me what my biggest problem is. I believe I need a man in my life to be happy but every single person I have been with so far has been the first person to show me attention. Simon, Greg, and Stuart were all coincidental relationships which for me, they were there at the right time. I do not regret my beautiful children, but I do regret my choice in Father figures I have settled for.

That's it, that is my main problem is that I always settle, and I have spent so much time trying to please the person that I was with, that I let my feelings be put to the back of my mind.

On Sunday afternoon I realised that it isn't only me that I have let get hurt so many times but also my children, and that makes me feel guilty again. From now on, I don't need anyone, and I think the kids and I will do just fine on our own.

A few days later I receive from Adam out of the blue.

He says he has been thinking about me and returning home for a while and wants to know if he could apologise to me and try to make it up to me for not keeping in touch. I messaged back to tell him that I am back home, but I am a little surprised that he messaged because I haven't heard from him for months now. We have been texting back and forth all afternoon, and he is asking if he can ring me instead of texting. I don't know why but the thought of hearing his voice is making my heart pump harder. I ask him if he can leave it for ten minutes while I finish what I am doing, and he agrees. Really, I just need a few minutes to calm my nerves. I really liked Adam, and it hurt me when he cut all ties with me. I am annoyed with him, but at the same time, I am glad he has got back in touch.

I wish I hadn't quit smoking last weekend, the kids have tested my patience this week, but this is the first time I have craved my cigarette fix. Damn you! My phones rings, and I answer it, my voice slightly cracking as I haven't spoken since the kids went to school a few hours ago.

'Hello stranger,' I say.

Adam makes me smile straight away when he refers to me as beautiful, but I am not that easily pleased.

'I am so sorry I haven't been in touch Sarah,' his voice is low and has me almost forgiving him already, 'I have no excuse for my behaviour. I knew from the start that I wasn't planning on anything serious, but I liked you.'

'I liked you too,' I butt in.

'I knew that I would be moving away, and I thought it would be easier to cut all ties,' he explains.

'So, what changed your mind?' I ask.

'I don't know, but I do know that I needed to say sorry and I would like to make it up to you one day.'

Adam sounded sincere, and I find myself reminiscing about the brief time we spent together. I had been on my own for almost a year when I met him, and he wasn't the first man who showed me attention. Adam was different to anyone I had been with in the past, and even the way we met was completely out of my comfort zone, and he knew that from our first date. I was able to talk to Adam about my past and not feel ashamed in doing so but most of all I felt comfortable when we were being intimate. I think because we both said that we weren't expecting anything but fond memories together, in other words, beneficial friends, meant I didn't need to prove myself to him. I didn't need to make Adam feel wanted, and I didn't have to put his feelings before my own. With him, I could be myself and not care if he liked me or not, because he would never be my boyfriend. I never understood that dynamic in a relationship before now, but not being scared to lose someone, is a feeling I had never known.

So much for saying I can do this all on my own.

WHY CAN'T I JUST SAY NO...

I am in my kitchen making dinner when my phone rings. It is Adam to tell me that he is planning a trip over and has asked if he can come and see me while he is on his travels. Initially, I tell him that I am unsure if I want him to be at my house while my children are here, and he reminds me that he has already met them. I cannot argue that I haven't missed him and since we started chatted again a few weeks ago, I have been smiling none stop. Even so, I tell him that I will think about it and come back to him.

'I have that book for you,' he says smiling down the phone at me.

I can tell when he is smiling. I don't know how, but I do. The book is a writing journal that Adam personalized for me by carving an ornate tree onto the hardback cover. Adam had originally shown me a book he had designed for himself, and I had asked him if he would make me one as well. That was months ago now and I had almost forgotten about it.

'With a tree,' I ask excitedly.

'Yes, I will send you a photo, but it thought I could hand deliver it if you agree,' he replies.

'I will let you know,' I tease refusing to make a decision straight away.'

'Okay princess, well please don't leave me hanging too long.'

I smile as we say our goodbyes and agree to talk the next day.

I am on cloud nine as the kids and I head into town for some much-needed shopping. None of us have many clothes left from moving back and forth and with the colder weather approaching, I think it would be wise to use my extra benefit payment for much-needed things rather than wasting it. I am also inclined to get myself some new underwear for when Adam is visiting. That fact that he has already met my children, I had already decided my answer before getting off the phone, but I wasn't going to tell him that. I would be lying if I said I hadn't missed his company although I wouldn't let him know what goes on in my head.

It is almost bedtime, and I decide to message Adam and tell him that I cannot wait to see him at the weekend.

Looking forward to seeing you too. I honestly mean that.

You should see the smile on my face x I reply.

I am glad a make you smile.

He honestly does, just a message from him and I feel all giddy. I need to give my head a wobble and wise up. Otherwise, I could end up getting hurt again. I am not sure I could take any more heart-ache.

The next morning, I decided to try and make things up to Katie for being a bit rubbish with her. She really doesn't deserve my friendship at times but in the same breath she is my family, and she only fell out with me because I went to Callum's Halloween party instead of her own. Katie can be a little funny with me at times, and usually, I would just let her talk to me whatever way she wishes, but she was snapping at my kids and being overly bossy towards us all. Living with her for three weeks really wasn't easy, but I am grateful that she took us into her home. I had baked chocolate muffins and been to the shop to get Katie's favourite treat. If feeding the woman doesn't thaw her out, then I am not sure if anything will.

Harry and Lucy head to the park, while I go to Katie's house. They don't want to see her, and I cannot blame them, so we agree that I will collect them from the park on the way home. Katie's house is only a few hundred yards away, and the kids know the way if they need me.

Katie makes me a cup of coffee and thanks me for the cakes and chocolate.

'You know me too well,' she smiles.

We seem to have sorted things out a little, and we are giggling at the fact that I slept with her Nathan.

I am telling her how ashamed I am feeling about it all and she surprises me by saying that it is fantastic news.

'You do know Nathan is my cousin?' she asked.

'No, I did know.'

'From my Dad's side, but it would be class if both my cousins started dating,' she says with far too much excitement for my liking.

'What part of him being married do you forget?' I ask.

'Oh Sarah, the man is a beaten housewife. Katarina takes every penny from him and forces him to treat her like some fucking princess. She is nasty and doesn't deserve him,' Katie is telling me what I have already heard from both my brother and Nathan himself.

'Even so, he is still married.'

'Only because he doesn't think anyone else will have him. She has brainwashed him.'

It is mad, I have known Katie my whole life, but I have never heard her speak about the Father's side of the family. In fact, she doesn't ever talk about her Dad and only talks about her Mother when she is bitching about her.

'Well, even so, I am not interested,' I smile to myself 'Especially when I have someone who has my interest.'

'Oh, who?' Katie asks me looking rather shocked.

'Adam and I are talking again.'

'Is that the man who used you in Belfast?' she asks.

'He didn't use me. We were never together,' I explain.

The next twenty minutes I find myself defending Adam to my cousin. Katie has made it very clear that she disagrees with me seeing him, or even talking to the man. I partly have myself to blame because before I moved back here, I was on the phone to Katie in tears with the way things were left between us both. Katie believes that Adam was completely taking advantage of me being recently widowed and basically used me for sex.

'Well do you know what?' I snap getting to my feet, 'Maybe I wanted to be used, because every proper relationship has turned out pretty crap so far.'

'You sound like a slag,' Katie snipes.

'Cheers,' is all that I can say in response.

Grabbing my bag, I head out of Katie's back door and walk calmly out of her back gate. I wanted to slam the gate shut, but I knew that would make me look like a child.

'You okay Mum?' Lucy asks as I head towards them both on the swings.

'Yeah, just a little stressed,' I sigh.

'Mum!' Harry giggles as I start to swing higher and higher.

'You forget this is the park I used to play at when I was younger,' I say.

'Wow this park must be really, really old,' Harry says.

He is getting cheeky, but I let him away with it. I really cannot be bothered to cook tonight, even though we have a freezer full of food, so I ask the kids if they fancy a take away for dinner. Of course, they jump at the chance.

It is Friday evening, and I have scrubbed the house top to bottom because Adam will be staying the weekend before he goes off travelling again for work. We haven't seen each other in over four months now, and I am feeling a little nervous about seeing him again. He has been charming and telling me how much he has missed me, and I have had the odd naughty message which has left me smiling for hours and daydreaming about what it would be like to see him again. I cannot deny that the sexual chemistry between Adam and I is crazy. I don't think I have ever been attracted to a man so much in my life. Well, not one that I ever would have thought I'd have had a chance with anyway. I am feeling like a big kid who wants the day to hurry up and end, so tomorrow is here sooner. It is only eight in the evening, and the kids have just gone up to bed. So, I head into the living room to put the TV on. There is never much on the box, on a Friday evening so I find myself flicking aimlessly through the channels.

I jump out of my skin when my front door knocks.

I don't get visitors, so I am wondering if it is someone coming to the wrong house again. Last week I had the door go twice, but both times it was some young person looking for the previous tenants. I swear the previous tenants must have been drug dealing from this house, but I keep my suspicions to myself.

I am stunned when I see Nathan standing the other side of my door with big black bags in his hands. He is crying uncontrollably, and I can just make out what he is trying to say. It doesn't help that the heavens opened half an hour ago and hasn't stopped. I tell Adam to come in because I cannot see him stood in the rain and sobbing like a child. Once I close the door, he repeats what he had said.

'I am sorry, but I didn't know where to go,' he says.

'Why don't I make you a cup of tea, and you can tell me all about it.'

It transpires that Nathan had a big argument with his wife and she has kicked him out.

'I am guessing she knows you slept with me,' I say feeling anxious about his response.

'Sarah, I had to tell her, she was all over me wanting us to have sex and to start off with I made excuses and told her I was ill or too tired from work,' he explains, 'I couldn't sleep with her because I want to be with you.'

I look at Nathan with pure horror and instantly feel bad that my face does all my talking for me.

'Nathan, we were a one-night stand,' I know that sounds harsh, but I must be honest.

'I get that, but for me, it wasn't,' he says.

I raise my eyebrow at him and ask him to explain himself.

'I think I am falling in love with you.'

Is this man crazy, we had sex once, and I honestly cannot remember most of it, and he is saying he is in love with me? I know that should have been enough alarm bells going off for me to say something, but I let him continue talking.

'Sarah, as soon as I did sleep with my wife, I realised that I have no feelings for her, for weeks you have been on my mind and I am going crazy with not seeing you.'

I want to tell him that he is being stupid, but the man is crying into my shoulder, and if I thought I felt guilty before for sleeping with a married man, I was mistaken. I didn't believe for one minute that Nathan would be the type of man who would tell the truth, not from the way that Ally had been talking about him. Why did he never feel guilty and need to confess all to his Russian wife six months ago when he started an affair while she was away? Why did he have to mess his relationship up over a drunken one-night stand in the first place? It takes two to tango, and I have just as much blame in all of this, as he does, and I find myself telling Nathan he can stay for a few days while he gets himself sorted. With any luck, his wife will have him back once she has cooled down a bit. Either that or I will have the Russian mafia knocking my door down.

'Does she know where I live?' I asked worried now for my safety.

'No, do not be silly, she knows where your brother lives, that's why Cal said I couldn't go to his house.'

'My brother already knew about this?'

'Yes, I have been at his all afternoon, I thought he had spoken to you?' Nathan says.

'No, he hasn't.'

CUTTING OUR LOSES...

I have told Nathan that he can stay on my sofa and I have warned him that I have a friend coming to stay with me. I do not know how I am going to explain to Adam why I have another man staying with me, but I feel like I shouldn't have to worry what Adam thinks. After all, he is just a friend to me. I do worry how it must look.

'The man I had a one-night stand with is sleeping on my sofa while you sleep in my bed with me,' somehow, I don't think I can get away with saying that without sounding like a tart.

All night I was trying to think of a way of explaining to Adam my dilemma, but nothing I come up with makes me sound any better than I am feeling. In the end I ring Adam and tell him that I am going to have to cancel on him.

'Are you being fucking serious?' Adam sounds pissed off, and I cannot blame him.

'I am on the motorway and only an hour away, what has changed your mind?' he asks.

I panic and make up a lie about how Stuart's daughter is staying with me, and it isn't fair on her to see that I have moved on from her father. I know I should tell Adam the truth, but I am ashamed more than I thought were possible.

Adam is annoyed with me, and he has every right to be. The last thing he says to me is that he hopes I have a nice life because he won't be wasting his time with me again. I end the call and break down into tears. Nathan is on the landing waiting to use the toilet, and he hugs me as soon as he sees me.

'I guess you heard all that,' I sob.

'No, but it must have upset you,' Nathan's hold on me tightens, 'Whatever he has done, I am glad.'

What a way to look like a total pig! I am clearly upset over Adam and Nathan starts telling how it is his loss and that I am too good for him. Nathan then tries to kiss me, but I stop him and tell him I have just got off the phone to a man who has upset me, the last thing I want is a bloody kiss. I feel awful, but I think this is for the best. No doubt Adam would have been off again and forget about me as soon as someone else catches his attention. I am too old for all the games, and if I am totally honest, I miss being part of a family. I miss being a wife.

I walked up to my brother's house just to get some head space, the kids are running off in front, and I have my music blasting away in my ears to drown everything out. I am angry with Nathan for leaving his wife for me, even though I didn't ask him to, but ultimately, I am angry with myself and vodka-fuelled or not, I should have known better. I am in my thirties and having a one-night stand, what must I be thinking? Ally and my brother seem to think that it is all worked out for the best.

Callum has admitted that Nathan was banging on about me to him, for the past few weeks and he had egged his mate into coming clean.

'Look the way I see it, is even if you don't want to be with him, he isn't with her. It's a win, win situation in my eyes,'

Callum says.

'What happens when she comes knocking on my door?' I stress.

'Nothing, she won't come near you, she might beat the shit out of him, but she would be all mouth to you. Sarah, you forget I know her,' Ally says, making me feel a little more at ease.

'Where is he anyway?' Callum asks.

'Went to his Mums to tell her the news and to see his daughter I guess,' I was only half listening when he told me his plans for the day.

A few hours later I say my goodbyes, and we head home. I have been checking my phone all afternoon hoping Adam would text me back, but the last message I had from him, was him telling me that he thinks he has had a lucky escape. I know I have pissed him off, but I was hoping he would have responded to my text. All I can do is apologise and move on.

When I get back to my house, Nathan is stood outside. He has been here a good hour or so waiting for me to return home.

'Why didn't you ring me?' I ask.

'I didn't want to disturb you,' he looks sad again.

'What happened?'

'She is taking my daughter away,' he starts to cry.

I don't need my kids seeing him in a state, so I rush them into the house and tell them to go and pick a movie to watch before dinner.

I usher Nathan into the kitchen and put on the kettle. Nathan had to go around to his old flat, but his missus has already changed to locks on him and put all his belongings in bin liners outside. Nathan's wife refused to open the door to him and told him that he would never see their sixteen-month-old baby again.

'Surly she is just angry and will calm down in time,' I say trying to reassure him.

'You don't know her like I do, she will be stubborn and stick to her word just to spite me,' he sobs.

'You can fight to see her. I know you shouldn't have to, but she cannot stop you seeing your daughter legally,' I say.

If you thought I felt like shit because of this whole situation earlier today, I feel a hundred times worse now. Not only has our one-night stand cost me the weekend with Adam but Nathan has lost his wife, home and now his child too. One stupid mistake. Now I wish I had gone to Katie's Halloween party instead.

WHEN WE JUST SETTLE...

Nathan has been with us for just over a month now, and we have had our first row a few days back. I caught him telling my children how much he loved me and that he would love to be part of their lives. He told Lucy that he wanted to look after her Mum and treat me the way I deserve to be treated. I went mad because my kids have been through so much that they don't need to have the added stress of my complicated love life. Nathan and I had a conversation last night about his so-called feelings for me, and when I told him it was all too soon, he went up the stairs and spoke to my children instead.

I do like Nathan, but I feel like I am with the man out of guilt so hearing that he thinks he has fallen for me already is a hard thing to listen to. He has been through very emotional few weeks, what with his wife sticking to her word and forbidding him contact with his daughter, but also with the fact that he is letting her message him abuse every day. She has even gone as far as to drag my children into the argument saying that they are slags just like their mother. I am annoyed when Nathan doesn't stick up for me, but I take it on the chin. He says it is because he doesn't want to make the situation any worse. He is lucky I don't have the woman's number because I understand I have hurt her, so will take all the abuse she wants to throw at me, but the kids are innocent in all of this.

Katie has popped around to visit, she has been here five times in the past two weeks, but before Nathan moved in, I never saw her. Not unless I tried anyway. Tonight, she has Martini and vodka with her and has told me she is in the mood to get drunk. I was shocked when she told me on the phone, that she has started seeing a twenty-year-old lad. She was stressing about the age difference for a whole minute before deciding that he was over eighteen, so it was allowed.

It is nice to see Katie with a smile on her face for a change, and if having a younger man has done that for her, then I think fair play to her.

'He came so out of the blue,' she giggles while explaining how she and Rick met.

'He is ginger too. I said I would never be with a ginger,' she jokes.

'If he makes you happy, who cares what colour his hair is?' I laugh.

'True, but I don't want no ginger babies!' she says sipping her drink.

By now we have both had a few drinks, and the questions are becoming a little more personal. I am glad the kids are fast asleep, and Nathan is out with my brother because Katie puts me on the spot and starts to ask questions about my Dad.

'Well I think he is scum and you should publish this book,' her words are slightly slurred as she finishes her sentence.

'Maybe, when the man is dead and buried,' I smile a nervous grin.

'Why do you give a shit, where he is or whether he is alive, Sarah the man is a child molester,' Katie sounds rather irate.

The way I see it is, it was all in the past, and I have tried to tell people about it in the past, and it has gotten me nowhere. I do think my life has been interesting enough for people to read but I will never have the thousands of pounds needed to publish my book, and I really don't want to open that can of worms just yet.

'Maybe when my kids are older,' I explain.

'Sarah, you can just publish under a different name, and none of the family would even need to know that you wrote the book,' Katie has a point.

'But Callum and my Mum both know I have been writing my story.'

'So?' she says placing her hands on her hips.

'I think you should do it, because you have nothing left to lose.'

Katie being drunk makes her bossier than usual, and we spend the rest of the evening with her telling me exactly what I should be doing and why. She has it all mapped out in her head. I am to buy the stock like I used to sell at the market and save like mad until I have the three thousand pounds the publishers are asking for.

'It will take forever,' I sigh.

Just then the front door opens, and Nathan, Barry and Callum stumble in through my hallway.

'Looks like you had a good evening,' I say as Nathan lets himself fall back onto my sofa.

'Yeah but Luke is a dick,' Callum Stutters.

Luke is one of my brother's oldest friends, while Callum lived here, Luke and he were inseparable but lately, they always have a bitch fit at one another when they are drunk.

Katie gets out her phone and rings for a taxi while Callum and Barry raid my fridge for more alcohol.

'Thank you,' Nathan looks over to me.

'She would have never let me out with the lads,'

'Lucky for you I am nothing like her,' I reply.

'I know that is why I love you.'

'Please don't.'

It is a few months later when things really take a turn for the worst. Nathan and I have been bickering a lot lately and even though he let his wife talk down to him, shout at him and hit him, with me, he acts like he is empowered and if I snap at him he bellows at me to not think for one second, I can treat him the way he used to be treated. I could never be that nasty but the way he is shouting at me this week has me wondering if the woman in question wasn't completely at fault. I would never condone violence, but I am ready to slap him, if he starts shouting again.

I know he has a lot on his mind, with not seeing his daughter but we are doing everything we can to bring Natasha home. Every Tuesday we are using his wages and my own money to pay for the solicitor fighting our case. Nathan's wife took Natasha to her parent's house in Russia a few weeks after they split up. Nathan only found out due to Ally seeing a post on Facebook, but luckily, we have been told that we have a case against her Mother. Natasha holds both a Russian and an English passport but as she was born in the United Kingdom, she is a British national, and the case is classed as a child abduction case. We have to pay more for a translator over in Russia, but it will be worth it if it means his daughter will be returned home. I asked Nathan what he is hoping will happen at the end of it all and he informs me that he is hoping he will be awarded full custody of Natasha.

'As far as I am concerned you are her Mother now, you will do a much better job than her own Mum' Nathan said.

'That is a nice thing for you to say, but it won't be easy,' I express my fears.

Nathan has told me that his daughter has been taught Russian as her first language as Katarina refused to speak English to her and with Nathan always at work, his daughter spent most of her time with her Mother.

'I don't care, she is worth it,' he says, and I cannot argue I would do anything for my own children.

I am at my brother's house having a few glasses with Ally while Callum and Nathan are drinking in town. I am not sure what happened while the lads were out, but Nathan comes back in a stinking mood. He is off with me, and I am infuriated when my brother tells me that Nathan has been trying to chat up the ladies all evening.

'You better not have been doing it too Cal,' Ally snaps.

'Don't be silly but watching him all night was class,' he laughs.

'I wasn't that bad,' Nathan slurs his words.

Before I know it, he has stumbled outside leaving my brother to chat with me about what had been going on while they were out. Nathan had been spouting his mouth all evening about how I didn't want a baby and that we may as well split up. I roll myself a cigarette because I have had a drink and I am so angry with my boyfriend for treating me this way. I wouldn't mind but I do everything for that man and treat him like he is a fucking king, and he has the cheek to act like a fool. I make my way outside where Nathan is sat having a smoke.

'What are you playing at?' I ask as calmly as I can.

'What do you mean?' he asks acting like he doesn't know what I am talking about.

'Flirting all night?' I state.

'It is harmless fun, get over yourself,' he slurs his words again.

Ally comes out to join us and gives my boyfriend an earful after hearing what he has been up to.

'Sarah does everything for you,' she says defending me.

'And what? She is lucky I am with her,' Nathan snaps before heading back into Cal and Ally's house.

'Is he having a joke?' I say shocked.

'Sarah, he is a dick if he messes this up with you,' Ally offers me a hug, but I am angry and head into the house after my arrogant boyfriend.

'I think I will get my two back home,' I say as I walk into the kitchen.

Lucy and Harry are still awake, so I ask them to get themselves ready and meet me back in the kitchen. By the looks of things, Harry is ready before I get into the kitchen and is telling me to wait for him.

'I am not going anywhere son, stop stressing please.'

REPLACEMENT BABY...

Nathan and I have been together for just over ten months now, and all I can say is I am so glad he is at work or asleep most of the time because, since last weekend, I cannot bare to even look at him. We argued a few weeks back when I told him that I was unsure if I wanted a baby. I am in my thirties and do not want to be like my Mother, doing the school run in her fifties. I understand that losing his daughter was a hard pill to swallow, but I have a feeling he only wants us to have a baby to replace the child he has lost. We have been fighting this court case for over five months now, and Katarina has somehow won the custody battle. Well, I say she has, Natasha, lives in Russia with her grandparents while Katarina is off sunning herself with some new man who clearly has a few pounds in his back pocket. Katarina is finally getting the lifestyle she thinks she deserves while Natasha, who is almost two years old now, hasn't seen either parent for the best part of the year.

All this started because I am due to have the implant taken out of my arm. The little plastic rod is inserted into the inside of my arm and somehow stops me from getting pregnant. Or at least it is meant to, but it needs to be changed every three years. That would be fine, but I have been told by my colposcopy nurse that I need to give my body chance to go back to normal and that I need it removed and to come off conception for a minimum of six months. Over the past five years, I have been having my smear tests every six months as I have had abnormal cell changes. I have had biopsies, and parts lasered, and had my biggest scare of all back when I was still married. After avoiding my smear for a while, I finally went and had my first smear at the age of twenty-seven. I was told that I had what is known as CIN3. This is where the cell changes affect the whole of my cervix. I was told at the time, that I was lucky I hadn't put my smear off for much longer as they could have been treating me for cancer instead. That was a scary few months I can assure you.

So, with Nathan banging on about wanting a child, I had finally given in and said we could try. If my other children were anything to go by then I should get pregnant soon enough I thought, but then he had to go and ruin it all, didn't he. I should have known that I couldn't truly trust the man, he cheated on his wife with me after all.

It was Friday evening, and Nathan had gone to my brothers for a few hours because he said my kids were doing his head in. They had been hard work and were both sent to bed at seven because of it, but I hate the fact that he can just walk out when he wants, and I am stuck here. I was in the house on my own when his phone started beeping. Surprised that he hadn't taken it with him, I ignored it. Until it started again a few minutes later. I was wondering if my brother was trying to call him, or his Mum so I picked up his phone, but it was a Skype notification. I know Nathan said about getting Skype so that he could talk to his daughter, but all he got was an earful of abuse from his wife, so he said he was deleting it again. Maybe that is her messaging again. I know I shouldn't look through his phone, but he has been secretive with me and half the time he hasn't even told me that she has been messaging and I surely have the right to know what is going on between the pair. She was telling him the other week that if he proves he is sorry, she will take him back. He said he would never go back to her, but I am wondering if the promise of his daughter is enough to persuade him back. I wouldn't blame him either, but I would never speak to him again if he did for obvious reasons.

I open the message but see he has three different messages from three different chats. The first one is off Katarina telling him that he has a slag of a girlfriend who is ugly and has slutty children and he knows he is better off with her. I can feel my blood pressure rise through me, and it takes all my strength not to reply to the message. I only stop myself because I cannot be doing with Nathan shouting at me when she tells him, which she would take great pleasure in doing so. It upsets me that he can stand up to me but wouldn't dare say anything back to her in my defence. I will only take it for so long before I do message her back. While I have the chance to copy Katarina's number into my own phone, just in case I may need it in the future. The next message is from a girl who calls herself 'Hotcake,' and whoever she is, she has had the pleasure of seeing my boyfriend's penis. Nathan has been messaging this girl back and forth for weeks by the looks of things. Having cam sex. The last message was last night when he was apparently really upset over his daughter and needed some alone time, so he slept on the sofa. All makes sense now you dirty little shit.

With telling Katarina that he still loves her in the first message and begging for forgiveness, to sending dick pics to two other girls last night, this is the final straw. I ring Callum's phone and tell him to keep his lying cheating mate at his house because I am fuming. Cal doesn't know what I am going on about, so I tell him that I have seen the messages his mate has sent to his wife and other women.

'Shit Sarah, don't tell me you looked through his phone?' Callum asks.

'Yes, I did, but did you hear what I have just said?' I snap.

'Even still Sarah, you cannot be snooping through a man's phone, it isn't on,' he replies.

'Callum, I get that, but the man has been messaging girls behind my back, I only checked his phone because it wouldn't stop beeping at me,' I am angry that my brother is taking Nathan's side, but I should have known better.

'The fact that he has been caught out means you can almost get away with it, but honestly sis, it is not cool to check his phone. I would have gone ape shit, had Ally done that to me,' he says.

'Difference is, you wouldn't be messaging girls,' I state.

'You have a point. I know which way my bread is buttered. I will keep him here for an hour, but you are both going to need to talk about it eventually,' he says before hanging up the phone on me.

I have never wanted to smash anything so much in my life. Yes, it may only be a few messages, but I have been through so much already, and the relationship with Nathan has never been easy. I am more annoyed that he hasn't been near me either, and on the odd occasion when he has, he is in and out within a matter of seconds, no kisses, no foreplay, nothing. It is pointless to even think about having a sex life and, yet the man says he wants a baby with me.

Sex has never really bothered me in a relationship, or at least I never used to think it did. My relationships in the past all had very active sex lives, so much so, that it happened almost every other day. With Stuart, it became mundane and turned into a routine, and Greg was drunk most of the time, but we still had an intimacy. Nathan and I haven't been what I would class as intimate in a few months now. Sex is just a way for Nathan to arouse himself. I have tried to spice things up, and it works for a night, before he is back saying that he is too depressed, or too tired. The man leaves me more frustrated than anything else, so for him to then be showing another woman attention has me seething.

As you can tell I forgave the man, Nathan turned up crying and somehow managed to turn the whole thing onto me by listening to my brother bitching about me going through his phone. The words Nathan used were, 'You hurt yourself by snooping.' Arrogant prick! It is only now a few days later that I can see how I was well and truly played.

All this stress is making me feel sick, and then to add to it all, my daughter has been suspended from school. Lucy has been playing up a lot since we got back here, and I am wondering if it is just down to her being in big school or if she is kicking off for other reasons. The problem is she will not speak to me or anyone else about it. I have been up and down from the school due to Lucy being sent home early after kicking off, and I argued that she needs some form of extra help at school. My daughter has been through so much, and I am frustrated that the school hasn't sorted out her counselling sessions yet. Harry is doing art therapy at his school, and that was the reason I asked for extra help in the first place. With Lucy at home all week I am putting the last few days behind me. Nathan has promised to show me more attention and never send inappropriate photos to anyone other than me, we will see won't we, but I think the trust is already broken as I have no faith in his words.

I don't know what it is but even trying to drink my tea has me wanting to throw up. Surely, I cannot be pregnant already. I only had the implant taken out three weeks ago.

IT WASN'T MEANT TO BE…

I found out that I was indeed pregnant, and it couldn't have come at a worse time. Nathan had decided that maybe us having a baby wasn't such a good idea. His reason behind his change of mind was down to my children playing up. Harry is good as gold at home but does spend most of his time in his room, whereas Lucy is very much in your face, arguing and slamming doors. Nathan says that I am their Mother, so I am the one in charge of them. He sends me up the stairs to tell them off just for making the slightest of sounds at times. Most of the time the kids being told off is warranted, but if I think Nathan is just a moody sod, I will stand my ground with him. As you can imagine, we have had a few disagreements this week. All the man wants to do is sit and play his Xbox, and it is starting to get on my nerves. He reminds me of Simon in that respect, and I am too old to have a man who gets more out of a game than he does real life. I have even tried to join in and try and understand what the fascination is with the games but running around a little screen shooting people isn't my idea of entertainment.

Nathan was asleep when I had taken the test and wasn't due to wake up till four o clock, the joy of working a twelve-hour night shift means he works all night and sleeps all day. That day I had woken him early because I thought he would want a bit of time to let the news sink in before he had to head out to work. By waking up at four, he would normally only have an hour to eat dinner, and then he would have to leave. Nathan is a line leader, so he needs to start his shift before everyone else and with that in mind, he is always out the door by five. I wasn't sure how he would take the news because it was a few days before when he said he didn't know whether we would cope with a baby. I shouldn't have worried though because he seemed happy by the news and even rang his mother to tell her that she was going to be a grandmother again.

Nathan's mood changed a few weeks later when I had spent the afternoon up at my cousin, Jody's house. Jody and I got back in contact over Facebook, and I had hoped to meet up with her while we were both in Northern Ireland, but she moved back here as I moved away. We stayed in touch over social media, and once I moved into this house, we had started to meet up for coffees. After not talking for a few years it was a little awkward, but once Jody had said the things she needed to say it was all sorted. I have found out so many things and the main reason she didn't want me to meet her at her own house, was because she worried and stressed over things that would never happen. Obviously, Jody and I have history when it comes to men. She feels there is a lot more history of forgiving from her point of view. Jody is still angry with me for marrying Stuart. She almost feels like I stole him from her. That is not how it happened, but I can see why she feels like that. Jody has also mentioned Gregory and saying that the night we met them, I knew she was into him, but I swooped in like I always do and took her man. The way things turned out I wish she had never introduced me to either men and I tell her so.

Jody has been with the same man now for a few years off and on, and they recently had a baby boy. Alex must be almost a year old, but that is still recent. It turns out she is scared that Billy will like me a little too much. I try my hardest to apologise for anything I had done in the past and asked for her forgiveness. That's when she drops the bombshell on me.

'Do you remember when we fell out?' Jody asks me.

'Of course, I didn't know why at the time,' I explain.

'Stuart wanted to keep me away from you,' she says.

'And why would he want to do that?'

I knew the two of them had been arguing at the time, but I didn't know why she stopped talking to me and moved away. Jody went back to Ballycastle to be with her family. Her Dad was ill at the time, and I had guessed that was why she moved, but I was told she must have changed her number or lost ours. Jody informed me that the reason Stuart and her kept arguing was that she had finally stuck up for herself with him and threatened to tell me everything.

'Tell me what?' I ask intrigued.

'You know he used to get me to shave his head in your bathroom?' she says reminding me.

'Yes, because I was scared of cutting him,' I say.

'I wish you had of, I am sorry Sarah, but the man didn't deserve you,' she looks at me with pity, and I am getting annoyed now.

'Stu used to make me suck him off while you were in the other room,'

I was stunned and didn't know what to say. The more time that passed, the more stories about my Husband were emerging. I knew Stuart had this weird controlling hold over Jody, but I didn't think it ran that far. Part of me is wondering if Jody did what she said on purpose to spite me, but I don't say anything. I keep it in my head. Just grateful that I have Jody back in my life again.

Jody and I do disagree on a few things at the minute. She thinks me getting pregnant was the worst thing I could have done. She and Billy have been falling out a lot lately, and at the minute their relationship is more off than on. Jody says having their son Alex is what has caused them to fall out so often.

'I don't ever regret having my son, but it did ruin our relationship,' she said.

Jody says that it may be different for me, but even she thinks this baby is a replacement for Natasha. I have gotten used to the idea now and finally warming to the thought of having this tiny bundle of joy, needing me. Harry and Lucy are getting older now and are a little more independent. I think having a little brother or sister will be good for them. It may even help to settle Lucy's moods out. She is brilliant with all the younger kids and has been asking for a baby brother or sister for years but always been told not a chance. Lucy was so excited when she heard the news. I have explained to my cousin that even if things all went wrong between Nathan and me, I was happy to have the baby, and I knew I could do it on my own if I had to.

I have my first scan in two days, and I cannot wait, but finding out about Stuart and Jody has me in a right funny mood. I am calm with my kids, but when Nathan turns up at home half an hour after later than me and starts bitching about how his dinner isn't ready, I blow up.

Nathan is off for the weekend, so I have no time-scale for dinner. I remind him that it is a Saturday and I have been at my cousin's house all afternoon. The man could have easily cooked for himself, and I reckon it is just an excuse to be lazy and moody. When Nathan goes in a mood, he goes to my brother's house, but he seems to get moody very easy lately. You would think he was the pregnant one, not me.

That evening after he has calmed down we end up snuggling on the sofa and watching a movie. Makes a change I think to myself. Nathan says he knows he has been a douche bag lately and wanted to make it up to me. So, a cuddle and Netflix it is.

'Your brother said he wants a word with you by the way,' he says as I reach out to grab my tea.

I ask him why? And he says that he let slip to Callum about my book. I look at Nathan with horror.

'I asked you not to tell him,' I sigh.

'He has told me to get you to delete it.'

Callum has no right, and I tell my boyfriend how angry I am that he has even said anything.

'I didn't think you wanted to turn it into a book anyway, what's the big deal?' Nathan sits up to reach for his own drink, 'You weren't planning on publishing it was you?'

'I don't know Nathan, but I am not going to delete my book, it has taken me two years to write it,' I snap but that is because I am now worried about seeing my own brother.

'Why, did you even have to mention anything to him, I told you in confidence,' I shake my head at him.

'Because he is my best mate,' was his response. I think the man forgets that I am his girlfriend.

'Bro's before Hoe's. Sorry,' he jokes, but I am smiling through anger, not amusement.

I take myself to bed, knowing he will be up all night playing his games, we can't all sleep the whole day.

It is nice having a big bed to myself when the man winds me up so much. I won't talk to him now until four tomorrow, and that will suit me. I will have to see his face when I wake up, but I am sure I would have calmed down enough by then, not to want to punch him in the face.

The next day we don't really say much. I am baking cakes with the kids when he wakes up, so he tells me that he will grab food on the way to work. I think it is just an excuse to get out of the house, but he won't dare say that to me, when I am still annoyed with him. I lied to Callum this morning and told him that I would delete my book. I know what my brother is like and he will demand to see my laptop files before believing me, so I am sly, and I send copies of my manuscript to my spare email address. I also save the book to a memory card and then delete the file from my laptop. I manage to tell Nathan that I deleted the book and to remind him that we have our babies scan in the morning. Nathan has said he will stay awake and come with me. I would like to think so too. This is his baby after all.

I feel like something is wrong. This evening I cannot get comfortable no matter which way I sit, and I had a little bit of pink discharge on the toilet paper which made me worry a little. Nathan and I posted a photo of my rather sizeable three-month baby bump on his Facebook last night, and our online friends are speculating on whether I am carrying twins or not. I do feel huge, for only being twelve weeks but we will find out tomorrow. I have messaged Nathan to tell him that I am not feeling too well and that I am heading to bed. Usually, I would stay awake until his break time at midnight and then head to bed. I am up every morning at six to have his breakfast ready after working all night. Only having five to six hours sleep every night is getting too me.

The next morning, I am feeling a little better. The uncomfortable twinges in my stomach seem to have gone, and I am excited to get the kids into school and then head to the doctors for my scan. I have been sent to Sutton health practice, which apparently has a pregnancy department that I never knew about.

Nathan comes in from work and apologises to me. He says he cannot come to the scan with me as he has had such a long night at work. I ask if he will just go to bed for an hour and let me wake him, but he tells me to take Ally or Jody with me instead.

'I thought you would have wanted to see your baby,' I say fighting back the tears forming in my eyes.

Pregnancy is making me very emotional.

'I do, but I promise I will come to the next one,' he says walking up the stairs to bed.

He didn't even eat his bacon sandwich. Oh well more for me I think to myself. I am eating for two now.

Ally has said she would come with me to Sutton Heath. She said she had been here with her sister before so knows where we are going.

'Bit shit that Nathan isn't here,' she says as we are in the waiting room.

'Doesn't surprise me lately,' and it really doesn't.

'If I was having a baby I know Cal would be at every appointment no matter what,' she says.

'Even if he was a little sleepy,' I joke.

I tell Ally about the twinges I have been having and the fact that I was spotting last night, but she tells me not to worry myself.

'My sister had six full periods while carrying Maddie,'

I can believe it because I have heard stories, where women have gone into labour, not even knowing that they are pregnant because they have had periods all the way through.

'Just mention it to the midwife, but I am sure you will be fine.'

As I am laying on the table being scanned, I express my concerns to the midwife who tells me she will have a look. She then asks me if I can empty my bladder a little so that she can see clearer. Now anyone who has been for one of these scans would know that the fuller your bladder, the better the results are, not that I am complaining. My bladder feels like it is about to burst. Ally comes with me, and I tell her that I am worried because the midwife couldn't see the baby.

'You will be fine.' she says.

We make our way back to the scanning room, and the midwife puts the clear jelly on my stomach again. She runs the scanner across me while asking again about the spotting I had the night before. I lay there when she tells me that she is sorry. The midwife can see the baby, but there is no heartbeat.

'I am afraid you are in the process of having a miscarriage,' she says as softly as she can. 'I am sorry for your loss.'

I look at Ally who looks like she is about to cry herself.

'Oh sweetheart, I am heartbroken for you,' Ally holds my hand while the midwife wipes my stomach clean.

'Do you need me to give you a minute?' she asks, but I tell her that I am fine.

I am told that I have three options, I can either take a tablet and it will flush the baby out of me but could make me feel sick, or I can have a small operation where I will be vacuumed, but that can cause complications. Or I can just let nature do its thing the way it was intended. I explain that I don't want an overnight stay at hospital so number two is off the cards and I couldn't swallow tablets, even if I tried. I am told to take it easy and to rest as much as I can. I am just nodding and cannot talk to the midwife explains what will happen to my body next and what to expect.

'The baby will come away within a few days,' the midwife says. 'Are you sure she is okay?' she asks Ally.

'She will be,'

Ally gets on the phone with my brother as soon as we are outside to tell him the news. Callum has said he will meet us back at my house. I am glad the kids are at school because I am dreading telling them the news as much as I am about telling Nathan. And now I am angry with him for not being here for me. Ally is being supportive, but Nathan should have been with me today, and I will be telling him how disappointed I am with him later.

I didn't want to wake Nathan up, and I leave him asleep until after two. He has work tonight, and I know how stressed he gets if he hasn't had enough sleep. Ally thinks I should wake him up straight away, but I explain my reasons, and Callum tells me I am stupid. Before I know it, he has headed up the stairs to break the news to his best friend. It is a few minutes later when he returns to the living room telling me that Nathan will be down once he is dressed.

'How did he take it?' I ask holding back the tears.

'He is in a worst state than you, and the poor bloke was sobbing into my chest,'

'That's awful,' Ally says as the tears start to fall from my eyes.

'I think it is starting to sink in now,' I whisper.

That evening I tried to ignore what was happening and invited Ally and Callum around for a drink. I need something to numb the pain and getting totally off my face with alcohol seems like the perfect idea to me, and for the best part of the evening, it worked. I was fine until I went to bed and the stomach pain started. Nathan had booked a few days off, and I was grateful for a change that he was here.

'We can try again,' he says as we lay down to go to sleep.

'I am not sure I want to,' I sob quietly.

The next morning, I wake with bad stomach cramps, and I am guessing that my body has started to reject my baby as I start bleeding very heavily. This is worse than any period I have ever known, and I am changing these maternity pads every half an hour. Nathan isn't much help because he is panicking about the pain I am in. By four in the evening, I am in severe pain and the best way I can explain it would be to say it was like an hour-long contraction. Whereas a contraction would come and go this pushing and tightening pain was relentless and at times was taking my breath away. Nathan wanted to take me to the hospital, but I tell him I cannot move. He then calls our cousin Katie and asks her to come over as quickly as she can, and to bring some more pads with her. Nathan then tells me that he will be back in a few minutes and that he needs to quickly ring work to say that he won't be in. The pain is getting worse, so I try and get off the sofa. I can feel that I am bleeding even heavier now, but I can hardly move. I manage to get on my knees on the floor and lean myself over onto the cushion. Just then I feel an intense tightening as blood starts to gush down my legs. I try to move myself, so I don't get blood on our new sofa and just manage to get to my feet before I plough into the carpet again. I crawl the twenty feet down the hallway and get myself into the downstairs toilet. I peel away my blood-soaked pyjamas bottoms and sit on the toilet. The pain is easing the more I am bleeding. Just then I hear the front door open, and Katie is calling my name. I try to shout that I am in the toilet, but I feel like I am about to pass out with this pain, although the dizzier I am getting, the more this pain is easing. Katie had seen the mess in the living room and assumed I was in the toilet. She opens the door, and the light hits me.

'The blood clots won't stop,' I cry as the pain hits me again.

'It will get better chicken, I promise you,' she says helping me remove the last of my bottoms and trying to help clean me up.

'Please leave me a minute,' I sob.

'I will be just outside this door, okay?' Katie says.

The blood clots are getting bigger and with the size increasing, so is the pain a few moments before each one comes away. I scream out for Nathan, but Katie tells me he is still outside on the phone.

'Please stop now,' I beg.

That was the worst evening of my life, and the pain was like nothing I had ever experienced. I was so angry with Nathan for staying outside the whole time, but I was so grateful to Katie for dropping everything and running to my side. I was sad that I had lost the baby, but I did also think that it was for the best as horrible as that might sound.

Things were never the same after that day, and I had already been thinking about ending things with Nathan. He changed, got very snappy with me and the kids, and the final straw was when I found out he had been meeting with Katarina behind my back. Losing our baby made Nathan concentrate on trying to see his daughter again, so something good came out of it at least.

I am a firm believer that everything happens for a reason and that I wasn't meant to have Nathan's baby. The midwife told me that there was no medical reason for me not to have carried the baby full term when I explained about my smears test results. She assured me that it was nothing that I had done wrong, and that sometimes these things happen, unfortunately.

After I had split up with Nathan, I decided that I needed some me time and, time with my children. The thought of running away was at the forefront of my mind, but I knew that I was only feeling this way because I was upset.

I have nowhere to go now either as my mother moved back home last week. She has managed to get a house off my landlord a few blocks away, and I told her the other day that had she still be in Belfast I would have been over in a heartbeat.

My main reason for returning home was so that Stuart's kids could have a relationship with Lucy and Harry but in the fifteen months since I have been back they have seen my children twice. I have even offered to take my kids to them, but there is always a reason why it doesn't work out. I can understand Stuart's kids being angry with me, but my children have done nothing wrong.

I am at my Mum's house while my brother walks in with Nathan, I haven't seen either of them in two weeks, so it is a little awkward standing in my Mother's back garden. Nathan has tried to talk to me a few times over text message, but I have stuck to my word when he tries to convince me to give him another chance. He even paid for twenty-four red roses to be delivered to my door. I accepted them, but I made it very clear to Nathan that I will not forgive him. I don't want to get back with him, but I am feeling a little annoyed when I find out that Nathan got back with Katarina. She is now living in the bedsit with him, and Nathan is back to sneaking around behind her back just to see his mates.

'You are crazy,' I say as they all start talking about it.

'I just want my daughter back,' he explains.

Even though Nathan and Katarina are back together, she has kept their daughter in Russia and is saying that Natasha is settled with her grandparents. I honestly think Nathan is being used for his money, but it is none of my business, and I spent over a year being trapped in their argument that I am done with it all. I wish Nathan all the luck in the world, and I hope he gets to see Natasha soon, but I wouldn't be holding my breath if I was him.

RELEASING BAD ENERGIES…

I have started to look after myself again since be-coming single. Eating better and drinking a lot of water each day and I have found myself engrossed in all the old spiritual books that I would have read in my younger years. I am starting to believe that I am the main cause for a lot of my heartache. Yes, it has been the men in my life that hurt me, but I have read a book which looks at how powerful our own thoughts and words can be.

This book says that what we say can manifest it-self into reality and we can almost cause our own bad luck by being pessimistic, I usually am a very optimistic person, and I always try to see the good in everyone, but I have spent most of my adult life saying that I am cursed. After reading this book, I have realized just how often I say the words 'I am cursed,' and I think I am going to start to believe in myself more. I know I am blessed, and I should be shouting about all the good in my life and not focus-ing on the bad.

My Mum has noticed my new frame of mind too and has said that being single suits me. I think while I am in a relationship I have let myself go, to stop any accusations that may have come up. While I am single, all I need to think about is myself and my children, which means a lot more time to apply my makeup just the way I want it. My children have said that I seem happier now which is nice to hear. I have met a few new friends, and I am now in contact with some of my old friends from school, and it has been nice socializing. My Mum has been a star and looked after the kids every Friday night, so I can go out and do something. Last weekend she got drunk with my family and had admitted that she only looks after my children because she feels like I never had the chance to be a teenager. She says she feels guilty about the way my Dad treated us all growing up. That doesn't stop her talking to him though.

I have removed a lot of people from my Facebook, either because I do not know them, or because we no longer talk to each other. A few family members who have never bothered with me have been removed too, just purely because I don't think they have a right to know what is going on in my life. Katie got a little funny with me when I unfriended her little sisters, but the last time I had spoken to them was over fifteen years ago, and I wouldn't even recognize them if I walked past them in the street.

Another thing I read in the book was about how you should get rid of negative people in your life in order to move on from a bad experience. Now, it wasn't saying that we should stop talking to someone if they have a bad mood for a few days, it is talking about people who are just always negative and people who enjoy putting either yourself or others down for their own amusement. Lucky for me I don't have anyone in my life like that, but I did tell my cousin about the book after she was bitching about her old friend Shaz who is always being nasty with her mouth. I told her that she didn't need people like that in her life, especially since she told me that she is pregnant.

Katie has wanted a baby for years now, and I am so happy for her, even if I don't think it will last with her toy boy boyfriend. I would never tell my cousin what I really think of the man, as it is not my place to say, but he has already been staying out on nights out with the lads and leaving her at home going crazy and not knowing whether he is laying in a ditch, or in another woman's bed.

Katie has been on the phone with me more this week than anything else.

I am at my Mum's house a few days later when I hear the news that Katie has suffered a miscarriage and my heart aches for her. I know what it is like to lose a baby and my own experience is fresh in my memory. I ask my Mother to watch the kids and run straight to my cousin's house. She isn't there. She is still at the hospital waiting for a lift home. It is getting late, and I need to get the children home and get them bathed and fed before they head to bed. They both have school in the morning, and I make a mental note to message Katie as soon as I get home and tell her that I will be around hers in the morning, once I have dropped Harry off at school.

The next morning, I wake up early and remember that I had forgotten to charge my phone the night before, I then realize that I said I would message Katie and I didn't. I feel terrible so as soon as Harry is dropped off at school, I head to the shop to grab her a box of chocolates to make up for being a lame cousin. Katie is in bed, so I leave her chocolates with her boyfriend and ask if she can ring me when she feels up to it.

Katie didn't message me for over a week, and when she did, she was angry with me for not being there for her, like she was with me. I explained that she was asleep when I called around, and yes, I could have called back a few days later, but I know my cousin, and I knew that she wouldn't have wanted to see me anyway. I think she is just trying to release her hurt at someone and unfortunately, it looks like it is going to be me. I can take it though and try not to be too offended when she starts badmouthing me to anyone who wants to listen to her. I get it, Nathan was the person I vented about when we lost our baby, but it still doesn't mean I like it.

A few weeks later things came to a head when I had messaged Katie to arrange a coffee afternoon. She had thawed to me by now but was still being rather short and snappy with me through text. So, I decided enough was enough and I would grovel for her forgiveness. I just want an easy life and having her as my enemy is anything but easy. I have stayed off Facebook because most of her post are about miscarriages and betrayal. She hasn't mentioned my name, but it was clear that it was pointed in my direction. She told my Mother that she is angry that I seem to be able to get over things easier and that I should still be a bubbling mess like she is. I understand that she lost her baby but crying all day every day will not bring them back. I think I am just a little thicker skinned than most people, but I know sometimes that must make me look like I am cold. That couldn't be further from the truth, but I cannot control how others see me, only how I look at myself.

I am sat around Katie's table when I let her in on a little secret. My silly head tells me that if I prove how close we are then maybe she will be a little kinder to me. I tell her that I have found a way to publish my book without hurting anyone involved.

'And it won't cost an arm and a leg like we both thought,' I say.

'How come?' she asks me, intrigued.

'I can self-publish,' I smile. 'The problem is I have told everyone that I deleted the book.'

'Please don't tell me you listened to your brother!' she covers her mouth.

'No, I was sly and emailed myself a copy before I deleted it,' I confess.

'I'm I the only person who knows you still have it?' she asks.

'Yes,'

I know that has made her feel special and she is the only person who I have told this news too. I know what my brother is like and if he knew he would go through the roof at me. That is why I have chosen a different name to write in. I hear many well-established authors do it.

Katie has been pushing me to speak out about my past since as long as I can remember, the subject doesn't come up often, but when it has, she has always tried to talk me into pressing charges on my Father.

I went home that evening feeling a lot better than I had done in the past few weeks. Katie and I have had our fallings out, but we never stay angry at each other for long.

BOOK BOTHER...

It is the middle of the summer and Katie and I have fallen out yet again, this time it is my choice of man that has caused our conflict. I had been thinking back over the past few years and feeling a little sorry for myself when it has come to men. I realized that with Nathan I made the same mistake as in my past and I had just settled for the first person to show me attention again. If only I had done things differently then maybe this past eighteen months wouldn't have felt like it was all for nothing. I don't feel like I have moved on really and I know it has only been four months since I split with Nathan, but I am starting to feel a little lonely. I do not want to be with anyone, but the odd date would be nice. I have been feeling fearless lately and even messaged Adam out of the blue. I am not expecting a response from him, but I told him that I am sorry for the way that I treated him and just wanted to say hello really. Facebook shows me that he has seen the message, but as I said, I don't expect a message back from him, because that was two days ago now.

Katie is annoyed with me for even messaging Adam, but it really is none of her business what I do. In all honesty, Adam was the only man who I can say I genuinely liked. He wasn't like any of my ex-boyfriends, and it was refreshing. Adam didn't care that I had a past, because yeah mine may have been bad, but everyone has their own shit to deal with, and I admired him for it. Adam also taught me to be a little more confident about my own insecurities and was the first person to make me feel completely comfortable while we were intimate. He seemed like the ideal man for me, at the wrong time in my life and I decided a message on Facebook couldn't make things any worse between us. Katie says it makes me look weak and desperate, but I don't care what she thinks about me. Katie also doesn't believe that Stuart cheated on me, which considering she never met the guy, she seems to be fighting his corner a lot. I think the woman just wants to argue for the sake of it.

When Katie goes home I decide to pop over to my Mum's house and wish I had stayed at home. It transpires that Katie had in fact gone straight to my brother's house and had told him that I never really deleted my book. Callum has been on the phone with my Mum saying that if he finds out I ever publish it, that he will make my life hell. He was very vocal from what my Mum has told me, and I am so annoyed at Katie, not just for telling my brother but to also because she just sat in my living room for two hours and never said shit to me. I am surprised that Callum didn't ring me to have a go, but my Mum said he wouldn't because he knows I have kids in the house. My Mother warns me that if I do have the book still, to make sure my brother doesn't find out.

'I do Mum, and I will publish it one day, but don't worry, I won't implicate anyone else in it.'

My Mum has told me that she wants to read the book one day when she feels strong enough to know the full story. We have tried to talk about it all in the past, but it always ends in rows. Least if she reads it in her own time, I won't be there for her to argue with.

I message Callum and ask him to ring me, but I get a reply telling me that I am nothing but a hateful liar and that I am no longer part of his life.

'Ignore him, he is just angry,' Mum says.

'He has no right to be angry. It is my past to tell if I want to or not,' I say annoyed at my brother's response.

'You do know that if your Dad found out he would probably kill himself, don't you?'

'Well I don't talk to the man, so he won't hear anything from me,' I say not caring what my Father thinks.

'Callum is very close to your Dad, so he is bound to want to protect him,' she says as if she is defending my brother's harsh words.

I receive another text telling me that I am poison and that a dark cloud follows me wherever I go, and that if I ever knock his door, he will punch me himself. It turns out Katie is still messaging my brother and has told him I emailed myself a copy and that I lied to him. She said to him that I had no intention of ever deleting my book.

She is right, but I could kill her for being so mean. Katie hadn't forgiven me at all. She was waiting to have something to use against me. All this because I got over my miscarriage while she is still moaning about her own.

I don't need people like that in my life, and I decide to block her on Facebook before she can cause me any more damage.

SOMETHING TO LOOK
FORWARD TO...

So, with everything being pretty rubbish lately, I knew something was about to change, and I was surprised when Adam replied to my message. Only a week late but I was left with a big smile on my face when he told me that he had been thinking about messaging me and that my message threw him off guard a little bit. Adam and I are chatting again, and it is really nice to have something to look forward to, even if it is just the odd message. I think he has just come out of a relationship, but I am not looking for that with him. I felt like I lost out on a good friend when Adam and I went our separate ways. We have arranged to meet up at the end of the month, but with the way, I called timeout on us the last time I can understand why he is hesitant to come and visit me here. Eventually we arrange to both meet half way and a plan is set in motion. My Mum has already offered to have the kids for me over the weekend if I need her to, so Adam and I can get a hotel room, and from the messages I had received earlier today, Adam must be feeling slightly naughty and is making me blush every time my phone starts beeping.

The next few weeks go by quickly enough and before I know it I am traveling to see Adam. It is crazy, but I don't feel like we ever stopped talking. He messages me most mornings and rings me for at least half an hour before we both go to bed, so I am feeling a lot less nervous than I expected myself to be. Excitement is rushing through me, but my Mum did make me worry last night when she mentioned that Adam could have planned this, just to change his mind at the last minute. If he did do that, then I couldn't blame him as I basically did the same to him almost two years ago now. Both of us have spoken in detail about it all, and I admitted that I lied to him at the time, but Adam had also revealed things to me too. Neither of us is expecting anything from this visit other than to catch up and have a memorable weekend but I know it is going to be a little awkward at first, and it is to be expected.

Adam has tried to ring me, but the train has just entered the tunnel, so I have lost signal and missed his call. He did send me a text this morning to say that he cannot wait to see me again and that his mind has been in overdrive. The man thinks about sex an awful lot, but it is perfect for my lack of confidence to have a man tell me how attracted he is to me. He has a way with words as well which makes me instantly imagine what he is talking about. He clearly sends a stir through me with his words alone. Once we leave the tunnel, I watch as the triangle of lines fill up my signal bar and try to return Adam's call, but it went straight to his voice mail. Maybe he is on another call.

Ten minutes later Adam calls me again and tells me that he is already in Cheltenham and that he will meet me at the Admiral Pub. I have never been to Cheltenham, and I am hoping this pub isn't too far away from the train station. Adam has told me to ring him as soon as I get off the train, which I was planned to do anyway.

Just one more stop and I will be there. Now the nerves are starting to kick in, but I know I will be fine once I get a drink down me. Adam has always made me feel a little more nervous than usual, but I wouldn't say it was in a bad way at all.

I ring him as planned and he tries to give me directions to the pub, I am lost already with his lefts and rights, but as soon as I walk to the front of the station, I see a taxi rank.

'I will just get a taxi to you,' I say walking towards the black cab.

'Don't be silly, it is a fifteen-minute walk at most,' Adam says.

'Try more like half an hour with my little legs,' I smile down the phone at him.

'I am shaking my head at you, so bloody lazy,' he jokes.

'The taxi is here, would seem silly to get lost when I don't need to,' I explain as I open the passenger's door to the car.

'Lazy, just plain lazy,' he says.

'Too late now.'

'Damn right it is too late now, you are five minutes away, but if I run now I may escape you,' he says laughing down the phone. 'Jokes!'

'You are lucky, or I would have slapped you,' I tease.

'Yes, but Sarah, you know I would enjoy it too much.'

I have gone red-faced just by talking to him. God knows what I will be like when we are face to face. Adam has always been a little cheeky with me, and I really do like it. His playful side I think reminds me to stay young at heart.

The weekend really was perfect from start to finish and spending the night with Adam was something we had not done before, but it was lovely to fall asleep with him and wake up the next day with him still there. We had gone out for dinner, found some live entertainment and stayed up most of the evening talking, amongst other things. Most of all, it was nice to be somewhere neither of us had been to and were able to be ourselves. I feel a lot more natural around Adam, in a weird way. I am not afraid to get hurt because I have had it all, and still came out the other side.

For the next six months, Adam and I are in contact every day. We ring, text and even skype each other and it is nice to have a man in my life, but him not really being here. Once a month we are jumping on a train, or a boat and meeting up somewhere new, making new memories. Having a long-distance relationship has its benefits too, but it does take a lot of trust on both of our parts. I have already decided that if Adam got with another woman I could not really blame him as we live over three hundred miles apart and have managed to see each other for a maximum of twelve days in that time.

Adam had asked me to consider moving to South Wales with him, but I took it as the light-hearted conversation as it was intended, but it has made me wonder why on earth I am still living here.

My Mother went back to Belfast herself last month and apart from Jody I honestly have no one here and moving back for everyone else wasn't the best move I could have made. Katie and I have fallen out big time, and there is no going back this time. She rang the social services on me and told them that I am going off all the time, meeting random men in hotels and leaving my kids home with strangers while I go off to have sex. The woman is in cloud cuckoo land if she thinks I am soft enough to forgive her. Transpires that it is all down to jealousy. She had heard about Adam and me and was annoyed that I hadn't told her the news myself. Katie still believes I should be with Nathan, but again, that is never going to happen. The day my cousin admitted to trying to find a way to get me into trouble was the day I had to ring the police on her. Katie and I argued on the phone before she started dragging our whole family into her argument by talking about our dead Grandmother. Katie says she is a bitch and knows it, but she says it is because of the way she was brought up by our Gran. I made the mistake of telling her that my Gran was a lovely woman and would never be so nasty and mean to anyone. Katie flipped!

Within ten minutes she was knocking my back gate through and trying her hardest to kick in my back door. Harry and Katie were clearly scared, and my crazed cousin started shouting abuse at me and telling me that this is all because I have moved on, without her. Katie was a big part of my life as teenagers, but she hasn't been part of my adult life in such a long time, I am wondering why she feels she holds this right over me. The police were called, and Katie had admitted to losing her cool with me. Saying that it was down to grief, but I cannot forgive her for lying to social services about me, calling the benefit fraud hotline when she had nothing to report but most of all I cannot forgive her for scaring my children. We are done.

Lacey has been spending a lot of time with us, and it is nice that she classes Harry as her sibling as well as Lucy and Mark. Lucy has been loving having Lacey as a big part of our lives these past few months and it has shown with her behaviour at school as well as at home. Harry, on the other hand, has been a lot harder than usual. He gets upset over the littlest of thing and has been refusing to do anything he is asked to do at school, but we are getting there, and he is now being tested for autism as he is showing a lot of traits during school. The doctor seemed to think it is linked to the loss of his Father which I can see why it would alter my son's way of thinking. At home, Harry is lovely and will talk to me all day long about what goes on in his head and the thing that is upsetting him the most, is not having a man living with us. Living with girls is annoying he says.

I have explained to my little boy, that we do not need a man in our lives to be happy and that I think I am doing a good enough job without a man. He agrees with me, but it is obvious that he is really missing his Daddy. I have tried to arrange to see Stuart's kids, and I have explained to them how hard their little brother is coping with things lately, but they don't want to see us, and I cannot force them. Unfortunately, Lucy thinks it is me stopping her from seeing them, but once she is a little older, she will realize that I cannot control how other people act, I can only control myself and how I respond and sometimes I even mess that up too.

A MESSAGE TO MY READERS...

Thank you for being part of my journey up to now, it is your kind words, and your continued support that has got me this far and I am so glad that I have been able to share my life with you. I hope you understand that now I am at a part of my life where I would like to keep a few things private, but I will tell you that two years on and I am finally the happiest I have ever been, and long may it continue. Adam and I have just moved into our new home together, and Lucy and Harry are more settled now than I ever thought were possible. They are both doing well at school, and we are all getting the counselling that we have undeniably needed for such a long time. Adam is the most supportive person I have ever known, and if it wasn't for his encouragement, I might have never published My Life in His Hands. He has taught me to be true to who I am, no matter what others may think of me, and that I should be proud of who I am as much as what I have been through.

This may be the end of my story, but with finally getting the professional help that I have craved for years, it has given me a lot more to write about. I am here to stay and I know that it is never easy to speak out about abuse and the patterns we seem to follow after the abuse has taken place, but once we get it out of our system, we can finally heal ourselves from the inside, out.

To look at me now, you would never know that I have had it so hard, but with health problems I keep under control and a brain which would have never switched off, my body was holding onto my trauma even if I was trying to let it go. I would like to say that I am getting a lot better now and writing is my main outlet for this.

One thing all this has taught me is that it doesn't matter how our life starts out. We have the power to turn it into anything we want it to be. We just need to start to believe in ourselves more and live for the moment, live for today because tomorrow is never guaranteed.

I honestly love you guys from the bottom of my heart, and I hope that my life can inspire not only you but others in the future. I am just little old Sarah but as you know I set out on a mission to fulfil my dream as an author, and I was lucky enough to sell a few copies, a few more than I had ever expected and that is down to every one of you. I will continue to write for as long as I can and looking forward to sharing the next chapter of my life with you all.

I am now working with a charity who support survivors of abuse, and I have been fortunate enough to be asked to ghost-write some of these inspiring life stories, so you haven't heard the last of me yet, I promise you.

'Everything happens for a reason' and I truly believe that from the bottom of my heart xoxo

SR xoxo

Printed in Great Britain
by Amazon